CHICHESTER

An Illustrated History

In this aerial picture of Chichester taken in the mid-1970s the outline of the city walls can be clearly seen. (*Jerome O'Hea*)

CHICHESTER
An Illustrated History

KEN GREEN

Published in association with

Chichester
OBSERVER
www.chichester.co.uk   ESTABLISHED 1887   1501 - 2001

breedon **books**
PUBLISHING

First published in Great Britain in
2002 by
The Breedon Books Publishing
Company Limited
Breedon House, 3 The Parker Centre,
Derby, DE21 4SZ.

ISBN 1 85983 336 5

Printed and bound by Butler &
Tanner, Frome, Somerset, England.
Cover printing by Lawrence-Allen
Colour Printers, Weston-super-Mare,
Somerset, England.

CONTENTS

ACKNOWLEDGEMENTS

Many people have kindly helped me in the preparation of this book, they include Mr Jim Shippam, Garry Long, Jerome O'Hea, Keith Smith, Dr Mike Nicholls, Paul Rogerson, Frank Hellyer, both Liz Neathey and Simon Kitchen at Chichester District Museum, David Bathurst, Councillors John Wilton and Anne Sclicuna, Gill Shone, Mark Roberts, David Rudkin at Fishbourne Palace, Geoffrey Claridge, Terry Roberts, James Kenny (District Archaeologist) Susan Millard at the County Record Office and Rodney Duggua, the city's Town Clerk. I thank you all.

In addition, two people, deserve particular mention, Rupert Harding of Breedon Books, whose gentle persuasion motivated me to take on the project and whose continuing guidance has helped the book to take shape. Also Arthur Smith whose help in proof-reading and extensive advice has exceeded all that one could reasonably expect from a friend.

I am grateful to the institutions who have allowed me to reproduce pictures from their collections, they are individually acknowledged in the text. And anticipatory thanks to Keith Newbery, the editor of the *Chichester Observer* for his help in publicising the book to his readers.

Finally, and especially, to my wife Sheila for her continual encouragement and practical support throughout, without which the book would never have been written. I dedicate it to her.

INTRODUCTION

IN RECENT YEARS there have many excellent books written about Chichester's past and it might seem reasonable to ask why we have decided to produce yet another. However, most of these publications have tended to cover specific aspects or periods in time. There has been no modern work for those wishing to find a comprehensive history of the city in one volume.

Not that this publication aspires to be such a project and it is doubtful whether the history of Chichester could be condensed into a single work. My assignment from the publisher was to produce a series of illustrated essays covering facets of the city's past that the reader could dip into at will. We hope thereby to provide an introduction to the subject that will help place the specialist books into context.

In many ways Chichester's history is a microcosm of that of England, most events in the country's past have had repercussions in the city and touched the lives of local people. As a result the annals of Chichester are a resource well worth study by those researching national history.

The sections have, where possible, been placed into chronological order. Determining which items should be left out has been infinitely more difficult than deciding which to include. The book will have succeeded if, through his endeavours, the author has been able to transmit some of his enthusiasm for the subject to readers.

Abbreviations used in Picture Acknowledgements

WSRO – West Sussex Records Office
CDM – Chichester District Museum
FRP/SAS – Fishbourne Roman Palace/ Sussex Archaeological Society
CDCAR – Chichester District Council Archaeological Resources

A Chichester
Chronology

500,000 BC	Boxgrove man.
3,500 BC	Neolithic Man.
AD 43	The Romans Invade Britain.
43	Vespasian sets up camp.
65	Fishbourne Roman Palace commenced.
280	Disastrous Fire at Fishbourne Palace.
410	The Romans leave Britain.
477	Aella's troops land in Sussex.
600	The Atrebates rule locally.
680	St Wilfrid arrives in Selsey.
680	Episcopal See of Selsey created.
875	Sussex becomes part of Wessex under Alfred the Great.
685	Wilfrid leaves Selsey to return to York.
895	The Danes attack Chichester.
928	King Athelstan authorises a mint at Chichester.
956	King Edwy's Charter to the city.
1066	Following the Norman Conquest the city is given to Earl Montgomery by William I.
1075	The See of Selsey moved to Chichester.
1075	The building of Chichester Cathedral commenced.
1107	Henry I grants charter for Sloe Fair.
1114	Fire destroys much of the city and the Cathedral.
1135	King Stephen's charter to the city.
1158	The foundation St Mary's Hospital.
1160	Fire again destroys many buildings.
1180	St James' Hospital founded.
1187	The second Cathedral fire.
1204	King John authorises a mint in the city.
1215	King John orders the demolition of the castle.
1226	Henry III grants the city 'at farm' to the Corporation.
1230	The Blackfriars monks arrive in the city.
1238	Emery de Rouen created as the city's first mayor.
1245	Richard de Wyke installed as bishop.
1253	Death of Richard.
1262	Bishop Richard confirmed as saint.
1269	Greyfriars Monastery built.
1269	St Mary's Hospital moves to its present site.
1295	The city's first MPs appointed.
1348	The Black Death strikes the city.
1353	Chichester created as a staple port.
1428	The Bell Tower erected.
1497	Prebendal School refounded.

1501	The Market Cross built.
1538	St Richard's shrine in the Cathedral destroyed by order of Henry VIII.
1541	The closure of the city's monasteries.
1602	William Cawley born.
1642	The Siege of Chichester in the Civil War.
1665	The Great Plague.
1672	The 1st Duke of Richmond born.
1689	St Pancras Corporation formed.
1712	Pallant House built by Henry Peckham.
1712	Oliver Whitby School opened.
1720	William Collins born.
1731	The Council Chamber built.
1748	London to Chichester turnpike through Midhurst opened.
1749	The Trial of the Smugglers.
1762	Chichester-Portsmouth turnpike.
1773	The north, west and south gates demolished.
1783	The Assembly Rooms added to the Council House.
1783	The east gate demolished.
1784	Chichester Dispensary opens.
1791	Chichester Theatre in North Street opened.
1801	Goodwood races first held.
1807	The Market House built.
1826	The West Sussex Hospital built.
1839	Chichester Theological College created.
1840	Bishop Otter College opens.
1846	The railway reaches from Chichester.
1852	St Peter the Great (Subdeanery) Church built.
1861	The fall of the Cathedral spire.
1872	The cattle market opens.
1874	Fresh piped water supply comes to Chichester.
1896	Main drainage laid in the city.
1897	Graylingwell Hospital built.
1909	Chichester High School for Girls opened.
1909	Electricity supply first provided – Chichester.
1913	King George V reopens the hospital giving it the title 'Royal'.
1929	Chichester High School for Boys opened.
1935	County Hall built.
1937	St Richard's Hospital built.
1950	Oliver Whitby School closed.
1959	Chichester twinned with Chartres.
1960	Fishbourne Roman palace rediscovered.
1962	Chichester Festival Theatre opens.
1974	Chichester District Council created.
1975	Chichester 900 Festivities.
1976	St Peter and St Paul's Churches amalgamate.
1980	The Granada cinema closed.
1981	St Wilfrid's Hospice opened.
1994	River Lavant floods.
2001	Bishop John Hind installed.

PREHISTORIC TIMES

T IS difficult to visualise more impressive surroundings for a township than those enjoyed by the city of Chichester. Sited on the fertile coastal plain at the head of a natural harbour, with the Downs as a backdrop to the north and the English Channel to the south, the location has enticed settlers for thousands of years. However recent archaeology has shown that, for the first inhabitants, the landscape was far different.

Early Man

Archaeologists excavating gravel workings near Boxgrove in the 1990s uncovered some of the world's oldest human remains. Until these discoveries the earliest known human presence locally was 75,000 years ago, during the Palaeolithic, or Old Stone Age, when Britain was connected to the Continent by land. We now know that primitive man first lived in the south of England during the Lower Palaeolithic Age 500,000 years ago.

At the time of these earliest inhabitants the site comprised chalk cliffs up to 100 metres high. As there have been no signs of habitation found below the cliff, it appears likely that their camps

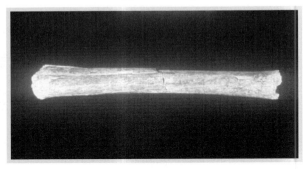

This inconspicuous looking tibia, or shinbone, is one of the earliest human remains ever found. Below: The stab wound in the bone from a horse's leg was inflicted by a man capable of using a spear to hunt his prey. (*Mark Roberts*)

A view of the chalk cliffs near Seaford giving an idea of the landscape in which our early ancestors at Boxgrove lived half a million years ago. (*Mark Roberts*)

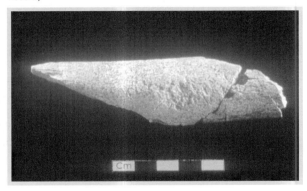

10

A picture of the Boxgrove excavations, showing the various strata deposited over hundreds of thousands of years. (*Mark Roberts*)

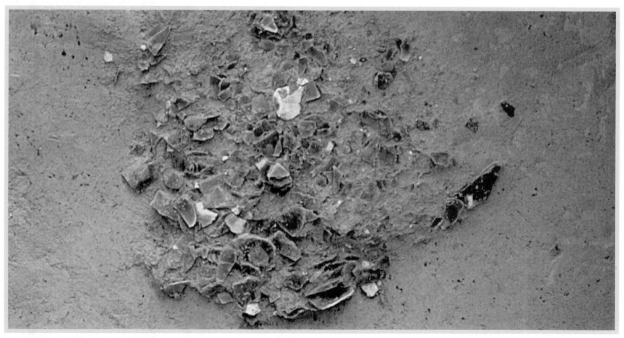

One of our primitive ancestors sat here chipping away to make a flint tool. The angle of the scatter shows how he squatted, legs apart, leaving the discarded flakes to be discovered half a million years later. (*Mark Roberts*)

were sited above in the heavily forested downland area. During the Cold Age, 480,000 years ago, the action of glaciers stripped the surface of the land and brought gravel and soil over the cliffs to be deposited as a covering over the site. It is in removing this sediment that the discoveries have been made.

The excavations, carried out by a team led by Mark Roberts, from the Institute of Archaeology, discovered a shinbone and teeth on the site which are among the earliest human remains ever found. The bone was 35.5cm (about 12ins) long and appears to have been gnawed at both ends by a carnivore. Other finds included a bone from a horse's leg that had been pierced by a hunter's spear. Scrape marks on it show that the flesh had been removed from the carcass using a

A member of the archaeology team delicately uncovers a rhinoceros rib. (*Mark Roberts*)

tool. From flint scatterings found on the site, and the methods employed in the butchery it is thought that these hominids lived in widely separated groups of between 25 to 50 persons. They were able to produce flint tools that they used to hunt and butcher their prey. It is probable that they were capable of co-operative behaviour and used language to communicate. The archaeologists have produced a reconstruction of Boxgrove Man showing that he was of stocky build, about 6ft tall, and weighed 13st.

As the last Ice Age, which lasted for about 30,000 years, approached, the inhabitants left for warmer southern regions. When the climate eventually improved and the ice melted away a far more friendly landscape was left and the Palaeolithic people returned. Evidence of their presence has been found, including axes, spearheads and arrows made from flint and bone discovered at many sites in the area, notably at Chithurst, along the Rother Valley and near Midhurst.

Neolithic Man

From around 3500 BC Britain was invaded by Neolithic tribes who crossed the Channel from the continent, originally they came from the

A typical Boxgrove handaxe of the type used for butchering large mammals. (*Mark Roberts*)

The Trundle: The defensive banks and ditches constructed by the Iron Age residents are visible in this aerial picture. (*CDCAR*)

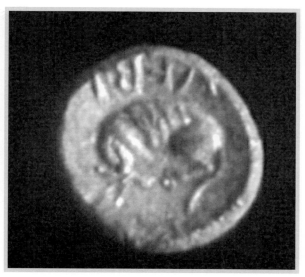

A coin found during excavations at Friary Gate in Priory Road. Dating from the reign of Verica, it depicts a curled dog in fine detail. (*CDCAR*)

Mediterranean regions. These people possessed greater skills than the native British, knowing how to clear land and to plant crops such as barley and wheat. They kept sheep, cattle, poultry and pigs and were able to weave cloth and produce pottery. These tribes built forts on many hilltops along the Downs. One such fort can be found locally at the Trundle near Goodwood Racecourse. At Stoke Down, to the north of Chichester, flint mines from this period have been found, whilst nearby their burial mounds or burrows can be seen.

Some of the nomadic tribes that roamed the coastal plain may have set up camp here. However no evidence of habitation before the first century BC has come to light within the area covered by the city.

At the Trundle, later Iron Age inhabitants strengthened the hill fort built by their ancestors. They constructed defensive banks and ditches and used the fort as a place of refuge to which where they could retreat in times of trouble.

The Atrebates

Among the bands of Celtic attackers that regularly invaded Britain across the Channel from about 600 BC was a group known as the Atrebates. This tribe, led by their ruler Commius, fled from the Romans in the first century BC to settle in the south of the country.

The Atrebate territory covered what is now Sussex together with parts of Kent, Surrey and Hampshire. Commius was succeeded on his death in 20 BC by his son Tincommarus. When, following a family dispute, Tincommarus (known as Tincommius until the recent discovery of coins bearing his name at Alton) fled to Rome in AD 7 he was replaced by his brother Eppillus, who in turn was succeeded in AD 10 by Verica, the third son of Commius.

Verica's capital, or oppidum, is thought to have been located near to Selsey. Coins produced at his mint, based at Medmerry, west of Selsey, and bearing his head have been found along the beaches between Bracklesham Bay and Pagham. Unfortunately coastal erosion has led to substantial areas of land that existed in the Iron Age being lost to the sea.

Indications of settlement within the city area dating back to the first century BC were revealed during excavations carried out on the site of Chichester market. Post holes were uncovered showing the location of three Iron Age round houses. Fragments of pottery from the same period have been discovered in the Chapel Street area and coins bearing the names of both

The Market site. The post holes of first century round houses can be seen in this overview of the site looking north. (*CDCAR*)

Tincommarus and Verica were found in Tower Street in 1967. These may indicate that some commercial activity, perhaps a market took place there. It is known that trading took place from Chichester Harbour with Gaul and other Continental countries at that time.

As a defensive measure against attack from the Catuvellauni tribe, who occupied territory north of the Thames, a series of banks and ditches were constructed to the north of Chichester. These are known as the Chichester Dykes or Entrenchments. Remains of many of these earthworks can still be seen. In AD 42 the Catuvellaunian leader, Cunobelinus, planned to establish power throughout the south and east of the country. Verica fled to Rome to appeal to the Emperor Claudius for help in defending the Atrebate's land.

THE ROMANS

THE ESTABLISHMENT of Chichester can be attributed to the Romans. Following the appeal for help from Verica, the Roman Emperor Claudius decided to invade Britain. In AD 43 four of his legions, in all about 40,000 men, landed near Richborough in Kent. After defeating the British at the Battle of Medway, they sent out expeditionary forces to overcome the rest of the country.

In the south the attacking force was the Roman 'II Augustan' Legion led by its young legate, Vespasian. After conquering the south-east of the country, the victorious troops advanced along the south coast. They found that the local Atrebate inhabitants, under their leader Tognidubnus, were friendly and offered no resistance. Little is known of Tognidubnus, he may have been a kinsman of Verica who took over command just before the Romans invaded. As the winter of AD 45 approached Vespasian set up camp for his legion to rest before advancing further west.

The Roman Settlement

The spot that Vespasian chose was a couple of miles east of the harbour at Fishbourne. It was on slightly higher ground than that surrounding it and was between two streams that ran to the sea from the Downs. In selecting this location he effectively founded the city of Chichester.

A navigable channel ran up from the coast to Fishbourne where ships from the continent could land. Recent research indicates that possibly some of the original invading army landed there. The Romans built a supply base with timber storage buildings and a gravelled road leading to the camp at Chichester.

Archaeological excavations in the Chapel Street area of the city have revealed coins, pottery and fragments of military equipment, including a short sword (or 'gladius'), left there by troops barracked in the vicinity. After two or three years the army moved on, leaving a military depot on the site. By AD 50 permanent buildings had been erected and Vespasian's camp had developed into a civilian community.

Tognidubnus stayed in power and was granted Roman citizenship, adopting the name Tiberius Claudius Tognidubnus. In 1780 workmen digging foundations for the Council House in North Street unearthed the dedication stone of a Roman temple that had once stood on the site.

This engraved bronze plate is decorated with a circular pattern of five dogs chasing a boar. Found in Chapel Street it originally adorned a Roman soldier's belt. (*CDCAR*)

Whist digging the foundations for the Council House in North Street in 1723, workmen unearthed the dedication stone to a Roman temple. It is now set into a wall of the Council House near to where it was found. (*CCC*)

The stone describes Tognidubnus as the local client king. It was almost unknown for a non-Roman to be given this rank and shows the esteem in which he was held.

Control of Britain did not prove easy for the Romans. In many parts of the country there was unrest and resistance to their rule. Here in the south, the local inhabitants co-operated with their conquerors. Clearly Tognidubnus carried out his duties and kept order efficiently. Possibly in gratitude the Romans built the palace at Fishbourne. It has been suggested that the building was the palace of Tognidubnus although the evidence for this is purely circumstantial.

The Romans split the land of the Atrebates into three administrative districts known as cantons, and the people of the western canton became known as the Regni. The township that grew around Vespasian's camp achieved importance as a port, a centre of administration and as a market town. It became the regional capital of the Romans, named by them as Noviomagus Regnensium, the New Market of the Regni. In time it became the most important town in the south of the country.

The four main streets of Chichester, which follow the points of the compass, are still as laid down by the Romans. The streams were diverted and joined to form one watercourse running around the walls. An inscribed stone, unearthed in East Street, recorded vows of loyalty to the Emperor Nero made by the local town senate in AD 59, showing that the town had its own local government in the early days of the Roman occupation.

The Romans were highly skilled highway engineers. Throughout the Roman Empire, urban centres were linked by characteristically straight roads. From Chichester roads ran north to Silchester, west to the Roman port of Clausentum (now the Bitterne area of Southampton), and south to the settlements at Wittering and Selsey. The major road in Sussex was Stane Street which connected Chichester to London (Londinium) and its construction started soon after the Roman Conquest. It took a route east from the city crossing the Downs near Halnaker and

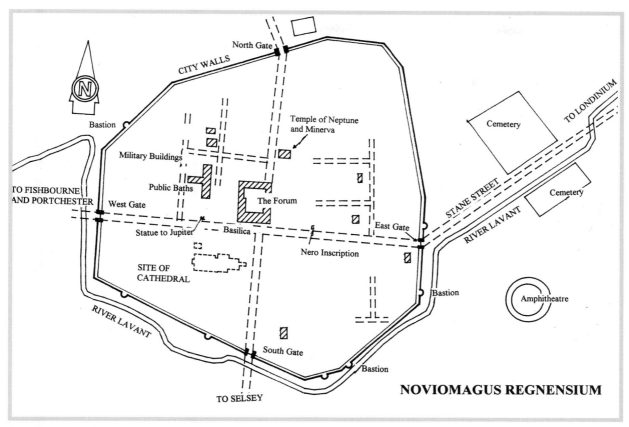

A map showing the city as it was in Roman times.

passing through Pulborough, Billingshurst and Dorking on its way to the capital.

By the end of the first century the city had a forum, traces of which were found in 1934 when the foundations for the post office in West Street were being dug. In a Roman town the forum was both the public square and a market area, serving as a gathering place and as the centre of civic life. We know that the temple in North Street was dedicated to Neptune and Minerva in about AD 58, paid for by funds donated by the Guild of Smiths (collegium fabrorum). Other finds show the presence of workshops within the city producing table wares, pottery and jewellery.

During the second century, the city was enclosed by walls. At first they were earthen ramparts built more as an expression of civic pride than to meet any defensive needs. In the early years of the third century they were reinforced with flint and stone facings. Gates were erected where the four main street passed through them and bastions were constructed along their length.

By the third century, in addition to the forum and the temple, the town had a regular street grid, a basilica,

A second-century mosaic uncovered under the floor of the Cathedral, possibly from the house of a wealthy inhabitant. (CDCAR)

A bastion on the south section of the city walls. Taken in 1961, the picture shows signs of many repairs carried out over the centuries.

public baths and an amphitheatre. The main public buildings were constructed of masonry, whereas the domestic buildings would have been half-timbered structures.

During work on the Cathedral in 1966, a mosaic floor from the second century was discovered which has been restored and is on display. Foundations of a large building have been unearthed in the cellars of the former Dolphin and Anchor hotel in West Street, believed to have been the Roman basilica. This edifice, which adjoined the forum, was used by the citizens as both town hall and law courts.

The city's thermae or public baths were uncovered in the Tower Street area in 1974, containing suites of hot and cold baths, a sophisticated drainage system and dressing rooms with decorative mosaic floors. The amphitheatre was erected outside the walls in about AD 90, here military parades and tournaments would have taken place. Its outlines can be discerned in the open area adjoining Whyke Lane. The Roman main cemetery, alongside Stane Street where the Litten Gardens in St Pancras are now sited, was excavated in 1960 and both cremation and inhumation (burial) graves were found there.

In the year 410 the Roman legions were recalled to defend the Empire against the Huns attacking it from the east. The Emperor Honorius advised the British to organise their own defence and Noviomagus was abandoned to the local tribes.

The visitor to Chichester today will find some traces of the Roman period within the city. The

The Tower Street excavations showing the Roman baths with their sophisticated drainage system. (*CDC AR*)

Chichester District Museum has a collection of relics, including many examples of pottery, coins, tools and weapons that have been found within the boundaries of the town. The city walls, which still follow the original lines laid down by the Romans, have been covered by rebuilding and strengthening in the succeeding years. The contours of the amphitheatre can be seen and, within the Cathedral, the mosaic floor of the basilica is displayed. The dedication stone to Neptune and Minerva is to be seen set in the outside wall of the Council House in North Street. However a visit to the Fishbourne Palace will provide the best evidence of Roman life and buildings.

Fishbourne Roman Palace
In 1960 a digger-driver, cutting a trench for a water main in fields north of the A27 trunk road at Fishbourne, reported that he had been retrieving quantities of building material as he dug. The Chichester Archaeological Committee were informed and, being aware of former nearby brick and tile works, they sent two

Fishbourne Roman palace. In 1963, as word spread, visitors flocked to see the new finds that had been just a few feet under the ground for nearly 2,000 years. (*CRO*)

A model of the Palace as it was in AD 75. (*FRP/SAS*)

observers expecting to find the remains of a tile clamp.

The building materials, wall foundations and traces of mosaic pavements that they discovered made them realise they were dealing with a major archaeological find dating from the time of the Roman occupation of Britain. The clues had been there to see as long ago as 1805 when a tessellated pavement and a column base had been found during construction of a new house near the Bull's Head public house. In 1936 a mosaic floor had been unearthed in a Fishbourne Road garden, but nobody had connected these finds as being part of a single building complex.

In 1961, when the land was under threat of being built on, trial excavations took place to discover the extent of the archaeology. Under the direction of Barry Cunliffe, the excavation team, mostly students, unearthed the remains of a building over 300 feet long, including seven mosaic floors. The famous 'boy on a dolphin' mosaic, which has become the symbol of the

Fishbourne Palace, was discovered during the final afternoon of the season's excavations.

By the time that digging resumed in the summer of 1962 the land had been secured by the Sussex Archaeological Trust. Over the next 10 years the site was fully explored and a protective building was constructed over the north wing to safeguard the exhibits and allow admission to the public.

It was established that the first buildings on the site were wooden shed structures used as military stores and constructed soon after the Roman invasion in AD 43. We now know that Fishbourne was an important landing place for troops and supplies from the Continent.

The second stage of construction included masonry buildings to the south of the main site dating to AD 60–65. Professor Cunliffe has identified these as the proto-palace, a residence that preceded the main palace building. Much of this structure had disappeared, leaving just the foundations of the bath house and some of the rooms.

The central panel of a second-century mosaic showing the 'boy on a dolphin' motif. (*FRP/SAS*)

The construction of the palace took place during the years from AD 75 to AD 85. It is one of the finest relics of Roman occupation in the whole country and is by far the largest and most lavish of the Roman residences in Northern Europe, giving some idea of the esteem in which the occupier was held. The materials and workmanship employed most certainly entailed the use of craftsmen brought over from the continent.

The formal gardens in the Palace have been recreated. Behind the box hedge a drainage channel can be seen. (*FRP/SAS*)

No direct finds have been made to confirm that the palace was built for Tognidubnus. Assuming that he was a young man at the time of the Conquest, he would have been elderly by AD 75 when the work started. However, there is circumstantial evidence that he may have its first owner.

Fishbourne was an important port in Roman times and many visiting dignitaries would have been entertained in the palace. In addition to their accommodation there would have been facilities to house the bureaucrats, servants, slaves and others needed to organise and run such a large establishment.

A Roman soldier dropped his helmet into the waters of the harbour. It was found in 1966 and is on display among the exhibits at the Palace. (*FRP/SAS*)

The palace was in use for over 200 years during which time it underwent many alterations. A series of bathrooms with exceptional mosaic floors were constructed in the north wing. Further work was taking place in AD 280 when the building was destroyed by a disastrous fire. The palace was never rebuilt, much of the usable masonry left on site was removed, possibly to be used in Chichester. The site became overgrown and eventually reverted to agricultural use until 1960, when it was so fortunately rediscovered.

Today Fishbourne Palace has become a major tourist attraction, visitors can see the elaborate mosaic floors and other features that have been uncovered. An excellent display has been created to outline the history of the Roman occupation and there is a fine model of the building showing the extent and magnificence of the Romans' work.

Vespasian

The man who founded Chichester, Titus Flavius Vespasianus, known as Vespasian, went on to become Emperor of Rome. He was the commander of the Roman 'II Augusta' Legion when, in AD 43, he set up his winter camp on the site which grew to become the city. (His son, also Titus Flavius Vespasianus, was known as Titus.)

Vespasian was born in Sabine, north of Rome in AD 9, the son of Titus Flavius Sabinus, a wealthy banker and tax collector. Little is known of his early years until he followed his brother Sabinus into a career in public service. He served as a military tribune in Thrace and later as a magistrate in Crete.

In AD 41 Emperor Claudius gave Vespasian charge of the Augusta Legion and in 43 he commanded the Legion at the Battle of Medway.

A denarius found in Chapel Street excavations showing the head of Vespasian. (*CDCAR*)

After the winter rest at Chichester, Vespasian led his troops to victory in 30 battles in the west of the country and the Isle of Wight.

Vespasian became a senior and influential senator under Nero, who chose him to lead a campaign against uprisings in Caesarea and Galilee. He was still away from Rome at the time of Nero's suicide in AD 68, following which the empire had three rulers within a year. In AD 69 Vespasian led a revolution against Vitellius. Joined by legions from Alexandria, Judea and the Danube, he led an army of 20,000 men. As they approached Rome the Vitellian army surrendered and, in December of that year, Vespasian at the age of AD 60, was created Emperor of Rome.

Vespasian was a popular ruler who set about restoring the city of Rome and its government, which had been ravaged by internal conflicts during the time of his predecessors. He died in AD 79 and was succeeded by his sons, first Titus and later Dominitian. After his death the founder of Chichester was raised to the status of a deity. Among his other achievements was the building of the Coliseum in Rome.

A marble bust of the Emperor Vespasian.

SAXON TIMES

The Romans left Britain in the early fifth century. The years that followed, known to historians as the Dark Ages, are particularly obscure in the case of Chichester. Life appears to have continued unchanged for some time. Eventually the buildings fell into disrepair and there is evidence of general neglect with rubbish accumulating, sewers silting up, and materials from the Roman buildings being taken away for re-use elsewhere. Eventually the town was abandoned as its inhabitants fled, threatened by coastal raiders. Only the city walls were left as a memorial to the Roman settlement.

The Saxons

Britain came under attack from Angle, Jute, and Saxon invaders from the continent who settled in various parts of the country. In the south, the Saxons formed the kingdom of the South Saxons within the area that is Sussex today.

Bounded by the densely forested Downs to the north and the sea to the south, the area was a distinct geographical entity. Under Roman occupation the region had been governed from Noviomagus Regnensium, but with the depopulation of the city, the centre of administration moved to Andredesceaster (Pevensey) where the Roman castle presented a formidable defence against any aggressors.

For this period of Chichester's history we have to look to documentary evidence to fill in the gaps in our knowledge. It is recorded in the *Anglo-Saxon Chronicle* that, in 477, the Saxons, led by King Aella with his three sons, Wlencing, Cymen and Cissa, landed in Sussex, fighting and defeating the local inhabitants at a place called Cymenesora. Local tradition has it that this site lies somewhere between Selsey and West

Wittering. Aella's name is preserved in Ella Nore, the small headland by Chichester harbour entrance. However, recent research suggests a

The remains of a child found in a grave pit on the site of the extension to the Alliance & Leicester Building Society offices in East Street. Archaeologists were surprised when carbon dating put this find into the Saxon period. (*CDCAR*)

site in the east of the county between the Rivers Cuckmere and Ouse as being more likely the place where the Saxons landed.

Whilst this section of the book was being written, the District Council archaeology officer, James Kenny, announced that radio-carbon tests on six skeletons, including one of a child, found on a site to the rear of shops in East Street had revealed that they dated to between 680 and 810. This discovery may result in the rewriting of the city's history. It has previously been thought that the city was abandoned by about 450 and that what remained was just the ruins of the Roman town.

It is a popular assumption that Chichester received its Saxon name of Cissaceaster, Cissa's Camp, from its connection with Cissa, youngest son of King Aella. Assuming that he would not wish to attach his name to a town that was in ruins, it is possible that he returned after his father's death to build the Saxon town within the remains of the Roman walls.

By the seventh century the kingdom of the South Saxons seems to have been concentrated in the Selsey area. A charter from King Ethelbert, who reigned from 681 to 707, to Wilfrid the exiled Bishop of York confirmed the gift of 'a certain parcel of land, in the southern part of Chichester'. If genuine, and some believe it to be a forgery, this is the earliest known reference to the city by name.

The South Saxons were in conflict with the armies of Wessex throughout much of the seventh and eighth centuries. King Wulfhere of Mercia became the overlord of both Sussex and Wessex in the 680s, but by 722 the two kingdoms were again at war. Mercia regained control by 770, during the reign of the last Sussex king, Ealdwulf. Finally Ecgberht of Wessex overcame Sussex, which became a province of Wessex and later a county of England.

The Evidence of Place Names
The Early Saxons were not generally town dwellers, instead their tendency was to live in small communities and many of the villages surrounding Chichester were first established in Saxon times.

The study of place names is a valuable means of obtaining clues as to the origin and age of a community, the Saxon word ingas, meaning 'the tribe' or 'people of', is one such case. Thus the Witterings (Wihthere's people), Ashling (Aescel's people), Oving (Ufe's people) and Graylingwell (the well of Graegel's people) all show evidence of being founded in Saxon times.

A *burn* is the name that was given to a brook or stream and can be found in the names of many local villages such as Fishbourne, Southbourne, Nutbourne and Westbourne.

Tun was used by the Saxons to indicate a manor or a farmstead. This word can be found in the names of Runcton, Compton, Hunston, Donnington, Merston, etc. Singleton was certainly a Saxon settlement, parts of its church dating from *c.*950.

The Old English word *wic*, denoting a farm occurs locally at Shopwyke (a sheep farm) and at Rumboldswyke, possibly a farm belonging to Rumbold. To the south of the city the names Birdham, Sidlesham, Mundham and Kingsham all reveal their Saxon origins as *hams*, or homesteads.

The Arrival of Christianity
Our South Saxon ancestors were, together with the inhabitants of the Isle of Wight, among the last peoples in Britain to be converted to Christianity. Canterbury had been an ecclesiastical centre for over 100 years and even the most northerly parts of the country had embraced the faith before it reached Sussex ancestors.

There was a small religious community at Bosham in the year 661, comprising half a dozen brethren led by a monk named Dicul. However they evidently made no impact on the native population and Christianity was not established in Sussex until the arrival of Wilfrid, the exiled Bishop of York, in 680.

Wilfrid, later Saint Wilfrid, had achieved distinction for himself as a learned churchman when he represented the Roman Church at the

Synod of Whitby in 664. A controversial figure, his wealth and extravagant style of living caused resentment, and King Egferth of Northumbria had banished him. After travelling around Europe he settled at Selsey in 680, where he founded his monastery on a portion of land granted to him by King Aethelwealh.

He was confirmed as the Bishop of Selsey by Cadwalla, the King of Wessex, who was himself one of Wilfrid's converts, and the monastery was raised to the status of a Cathedral. Opinions vary as to whether it was sited at Church Norton or on a site now lost to the sea.

After the death of Egferth in 685, Wilfrid returned to the north of the country where he founded both Hexham Abbey and Ripon Cathedral, in which he was buried after his death in 709. Selsey was established as an Ecclesiastical See with its own line of bishops. The first of these was Eadberht, the former abbot; with the exception of Ethelgar who became Archbishop of Canterbury in 953, we know little about succeeding bishops other than their names, gleaned from various charters and documents.

The Saxon Burh

The *Anglo-Saxon Chronicle* tells that, in 895, a marauding Danish army attacked many towns in the south. As they turned homewards from attacking Exeter they harassed the South Saxons near Chichester, whose burgesses 'put them to flight and slew many hundreds at them and took some of their ships'. Traditionally it is held that this battle took place at Kingley Vale in the

A coin minted in Chichester in the reign of King Edgar, 958–975. (*CDCAR*)

Downs to the north of Chichester.

By 875 Sussex had became part of Wessex, the kingdom of Alfred the Great. He ordered that in Chichester the walls should be rebuilt and the town designated as one of the burhs, or fortified towns, that he formed around his kingdom.

The town was of sufficient importance by the year 928 for coins to be produced here at a mint sanctioned by King Athelstan. The south gate is mentioned in a document dated 930, implying that the walls were in a state of repair at that time. A charter given to the 'brethren residing in Chichester' from King Edwy in 956 confirms that a monastery existed within the city.

The Domesday Book, besides being a survey of the state of affairs at the time that it was published, also provides details of the country before the coming of the Normans. It records that there were 300 houses in Chichester in the time of Edward the Confessor. Fifty-one of these houses were owned by Roger, Earl Godwin, the father of King Harold. It is therefore difficult not to believe that many men from Chichester were present at Hastings fighting for the ill-fated king.

Little evidence remains within the city of the Saxon age. One legacy is the layout of the city's streets which, apart from the four main Roman thoroughfares, remains largely as set out by the Saxons. The nave of St Olave's Church in North Street, now the SPCK bookshop, is of Saxon construction.

THE NORMAN CITY

ONE date known by all is that of the Battle of Hastings in 1066. What is often not appreciated is the profound and lasting effect that the Conquest had upon both the nation and its people.

William the Conqueror was a great reformer. Hardly ever before or since has a national culture been so quickly submerged as that of Anglo-Saxon England in the 11th century. The country's official language, art and architecture were all replaced by those of the continental invader. Changes were made to the laws of the land and in government. Throughout the country a vast programme of building was instituted. The Normans built new castles, abbeys and churches, at the same time demolishing many older buildings.

The Normans

The Conqueror's zeal for reform was nowhere more apparent than in the Church. Many senior clergy were displaced, their places filled by the king's countrymen. These included the replacement of Stigand, Archbishop of Canterbury, by Lanfranc, Abbot of Caen, and locally Aethelric the Bishop of Selsey by the king's chaplain, also named Stigand.

In 1075 Archbishop Lanfranc presided over the Great Synod of London. Among the decisions it made was the removal of many bishoprics from less important rural townships to the urban centres of local government. As a result, many of today's Cathedral cities were created, the See of Elmham was transferred to Norwich, that of Lichfield to Chester, Salisbury replaced Sherbourne and, significantly for Chichester, Stigand's seat was moved there from Selsey. In William of Malmesbury's account we are told that, when he moved his episcopal seat from Selsey, Bishop Stigand displaced a 'nunnery of monks' in Chichester. This probably referred to the monastery that had existed in the time of King Edwy.

William's feudal system of government subdivided the country into separate units or manors which he distributed among his loyal followers. Sussex was divided into six Rapes, each within the lordship of a baron. The Rape of Chichester was bestowed, together with that of Arundel and the Earldom of Shrewsbury, to Roger de Montgomery as a reward from a grateful monarch to a subject who had been a brave leader at Hastings.

When Earl Roger died, in 1094, the Earldom of Chichester passed to his eldest son Hugh de Bellesme, who was succeeded by his brother Robert. In 1102 Robert joined the rebel barons who attempted to overthrow Henry II. The plot failed and he was deprived of the Earldom. Henry granted the city to his second wife Queen Adeliza in 1121. After Henry's death Adeliza remarried. Her husband, William d'Aubigny, became the 4th Earl of Chichester, followed by his son William in 1176. On his death, in 1193, the city again returned to the possession of the king.

Fire seems to have been a constant threat during this period. On 5 May 1114, a disastrous fire spread through the city when many of the timber buildings were lost. In 1160 fire devastated the market place and a serious outbreak in 1187 did substantial damage to the Cathedral.

The Normans divided the Diocese of Chichester into two archdeaconries, Chichester and Lewes. These were sub-divided into

An impression of the castle in winter by artist Mike Codd. (*CDC*)

deaneries, which were in turn broken down into parishes. These divisions have endured almost unchanged until the present time. The Pallant area of Chichester together with the parish of Pagham, came under the jurisdiction of the Archbishop of Canterbury.

The Castle

William conferred on his barons the right to build castles. Over 2,500 are known to have been built throughout the land. They formed military garrisons and the centres of local authority.

In Chichester the new Earl built a castle in the north-east quarter of the city. It was a motte and bailey type of structure, intended to be a stronghold in case the city was attacked. The mound of the castle still survives in what is now Priory Park, the lack of foundations show that the castle keep was of timber construction.

Roger's main residence in Sussex was the stone-built castle that he constructed at Arundel.

We know that, by 1142, there was a chapel within the outer walls of the Chichester Castle. There are accounts of quantities of goods and stores being purchased to provision the garrison. Supplies of bacon, beans, barley and weapons show that the occupants were prepared to withstand quite a long siege should the occasion arise.

The various sums that were spent on the upkeep and repair of the castle during the 12th century give an idea of the importance of the establishment in the defence of this part of Sussex against possible attack from seaborne assailants.

In 1215, King John gave instructions for the castle to be demolished. He feared that, in the event of invasion by the French, it could fall into

Visitors to Priory Park who laze on the grass banks may not always appreciate the Norman origins of the castle mound.

their hands. His fears were justified in 1216 when Prince Louis, the French Dauphin, invaded England and took the castle. It was recaptured the following year, after John's death, and the demolition was finally carried out.

In 1198 the Sheriff of Sussex had been allowed £5.10s to repair the gaol which is thought to have been sited within the castle precincts. Following the demolition of the castle this building was retained. In 1223 a house was built for the gaoler who received a yearly wage of £3 0s 10d (or 2d a day). For the next 40 years it served as the common gaol for Sussex. By 1237 it was receiving prisoners sent to it by the king's command, although after then records cease. From then on many Sussex prisoners were held in Guildford Goal. This may be because the posts of Sheriff of both Sussex and Surrey were often held simultaneously by the same person during this period.

The castle mound remained after the demolition. It was put to military use once again in 1642, when during the Siege of Chichester a defensive battery was sited there. Nowadays the mound provides an excellent vantage point for visitors and cricket spectators.

The Early Cathedral

Earl Roger de Montgomery granted the south-west quadrant of the city to the Bishop of Chichester. To this day, in addition to the Cathedral, it still contains the Bishop's Palace, the Vicars' Hall, the Prebendal School and the dwellings of many of the Cathedral's senior clergy.

For many years it has been thought that Ralph Luffa, Chichester's third bishop, started the

The cushion capital to this column in the main aisle of the Cathedral is typical of the Norman style.

This doorway in the south wall of the Cathedral, with its characteristic dog tooth decoration is a relic of the earliest building.

construction of the Cathedral soon after his appointment in 1091. However, Tim Tatton-Brown has recently shown that, in fact, the work started soon after the arrival of Stigand in 1075.

Chichester's second bishop was Godfrey, of whom we know little. In 1829 workmen discovered Godfrey's stone coffin in Paradise, the Cathedral graveyard. On the bishop's chest was a small leaden cross which was inscribed with an absolution, granted by the Pope. Unfortunately the nature of the offence which required this pardon is not recorded.

In the early 12th century, the construction of new cathedrals, castles and other buildings was taking place throughout the country. This no doubt led to shortages of both good building stone and skilled labour. In Chichester, the decision was made to use stone from Quarr on the Isle of Wight; this was probably not the preferred option and may have led to defects in construction that caused problems in later years.

The Cathedral was sufficiently complete by 1108 to be dedicated to St Peter, as had been the former monastery on the site.

In the fire that spread through the city, in 1114, the wooden roof of the Cathedral was destroyed. Bishop Ralph was undeterred and immediately commenced the task of rebuilding. It was repaired and back in use before his death in 1125.

In 1180, Seffrid II was appointed bishop, having previously been archdeacon and dean. He was in office in 1187 when fire, again, did substantial damage to the Cathedral. It was repaired and this time the roof was rebuilt with stone vaulting. The work was completed in 1199 when the church was rededicated to the Holy Trinity in a service attended by six bishops.

The 12th-century stone carving depicting the Raising of Lazurus.

Christ arriving at Bethany. Mary and Martha greet Christ.

Although King John was possibly the most unpopular of England's monarchs, he proved a generous benefactor to Chichester. In 1204 the king gave Bishop Simon de Wells, who was one of his favourites, permission to build on a strip of land between the Cathedral and West Street. The buildings, which were known as Bishop's Row, in addition to houses contained three inns, a slaughterhouse and a timber yard. All were demolished between 1848–52 to be replaced by a line of trees.

Possibly the Cathedral's greatest treasures are the two carved stone panels known as the Chichester Reliefs. These were discovered when panelling above the choir stalls was removed in 1829. Fortunately they were removed to their present position in the south choir aisle and thus escaped destruction when the spire collapsed in

1861. They depict Christ arriving at Bethany and the Raising of Lazarus, it is thought that they were carved in the early 12th century and were possibly part of eight panels forming a frieze. They rank among the greatest artistic works from the Romanesque period.

The Cathedral is a lasting monument to the Norman period with many of the original internal features still to be seen.

St Cyriac's Chapel

One memorial to the Norman Age that has survived is the name of St Cyriac which is now attached to a car park on land off Chapel Street. Some time before his death in 1094, Earl Roger founded a chantry chapel on the site, then known as Paris Lane, which housed a priest whose task was to pray for the soul of Roger and his ancestors.

The chapel was dedicated to St Cyriac, a fourth-century saint who was a favourite of the Normans at that time. By 1247 the chapel was the abode of a hermit to whom Dean Geoffrey left a bequest of one penny a year. When Henry III visited the city in 1269 he made an endowment of 50 marks to the chapel and a further five marks to support the chaplain, Stephen de Midhurst.

In 1405 the chapel was again in use as a hermitage, Bishop Robert Reade granting indulgences to anyone who would help to support Richard Petevine, 'the hermit of the chapel of St Cyriac'. Religious use of the chapel had ceased by 1579 when it was in use as a barn. By 1820 the building was in a ruinous condition. It was demolished and the site became part of the garden of the house, now known as Fernleigh, which had been built in 1807.

THE MEDIAEVAL CITY

CHICHESTER'S advantageous position between the Downs and the sea led to it becoming an important centre for trades dependent upon agricultural produce such as tanning, brewing and the production of woollen cloth. In 1204, with the issue of the county's reformed coinage, King John chose the city to be one of the boroughs in which money could be minted. However, this privilege was short-lived as, following a national outbreak of forgery in 1207, many mints were closed, Chichester among them. As the seat of the bishop, the city was also the centre of religious life for Sussex, the county being coterminous with the Diocese of Chichester.

Although Chichester had no direct access to the sea its proximity to the harbour led, in 1275, to it being designated as a port by Edward I. This enabled the king to levy taxes on imports and exports. Ships berthed at Dellquay, Itchenor, Birdham, Bosham and Fishbourne. The main import in the 13th century was wine on which tunnage was levied. Exports included cargoes of hides, bacon, corn and cheese, however by far the principal trade was in wool. In 1353 the city became a 'staple port' which was one authorised to deal with the export of wool. In addition the citizens were granted charters giving them rights to control fishing within the harbour and to levy fees on those using the port.

Markets and Fairs

In the early Middle Ages the holding of markets and fairs were important occasions for both the townspeople and those living in surrounding villages. They could only be held with the direct authority of the king. In common with most of the larger towns and cities in the country, Chichester sought charters to hold such events which, when granted, were of importance to local landowners who received the tolls paid by tradesmen using the markets. The establishment of a market also encouraged trade which was itself both necessary and desirable.

Henry I granted permission in 1107 to Bishop Ralph to hold a fair each year for eight days on the feast of St Faith, 6 October. This fair became known as Sloe Fair after a tree in the field outside of the north gate where it was held. It is still an annual event although its nature has changed in the succeeding years and it now lasts for only one day.

The Merchants' Guild

With the exception of Sloe Fair, control of markets and fairs was vested in the city's Borough and Merchants' Guild, a body comprising elected burgesses of the city.

The earliest mention of the Guild is in the royal charter granted to the burgesses by King Stephen. The charter is dated about 1135 and in it Stephen refers to earlier rights granted to the city by his grandfather King William. Further charters were granted by Henry II in 1155, which gave additional powers to the Guild. The brethren and, surprisingly, the sisters of the Guild elected their master and four wardens each year. In addition to controlling trading and fairs within the city, the Guild monitored the numbers of apprentices and settled quarrels between traders.

In 1226 Henry III granted the city 'at farm' to the citizens which gave them the right of collecting local taxes in return for a yearly fee of £36. However, the king kept the duties collected on wool and hides for himself.

As in many mediaeval towns, the Merchants' Guilds evolved into the Common Council for the city, appointing a mayor, aldermen, bailiffs and other officers. The first mayor was Emery de Rouen who took office in 1238. When the first Model Parliament was called by Edward I at Westminster in November 1295, the council elected two representatives from amongst their membership. William of Eartham and Clement of Asdean were the first Members of Parliament, Walter the Spicer and John from the Pallant succeeded them in 1298.

The Crypt

The building in South Street that is popularly known as the Crypt should rightly be called an undercroft. The structure was originally part of a guildhall that is known to have been on the site in the 12th century. This building was demolished in 1396 to make way for the new Vicars'

Hall. Records show that the dean, John de Maidenhith, laid the first stone at a ceremony on 6 March 1396.

The undercroft, which is today a restaurant, was probably used as a cellar for storage. In 1661 it was leased to the landlord of the White Horse Inn, opposite in South Street, who used it as a cellar. However, in 1686, one of the resident vicars complained that the then landlord, Mr Booker, was keeping swine there. Subsequently the building has had varied uses, as a horticultural store, an antique dealer's shop, and, for a brief time in the 19th century, as the city's post office before being converted to its present use in 1957.

Above the Crypt, the Vicars' Hall was the residence for the Cathedral vicars who ate and slept there. It has recently been refurbished and is used as a meeting hall which today is reached from an entrance in the Cathedral grounds. In

The Vicars' Hall in West Street. Today it serves as a meeting room for Cathedral and other functions.

The earlier crypt, or undercroft of the Vicars' Hall has also been used for many purposes in the past, it is seen here before conversion to its present use as a restaurant.

the hall's south wall can be seen a recess from which readings from the Bible were made to the vicars as they ate their meals without speaking.

The Black Death

In 1348 the bubonic plague, or the Black Death as it came to be known, reached England. The first outbreak was in Dorset, initially borne by flea-ridden rats. It was highly contagious and by 1349 had devastated the whole country. It is estimated that one third of the population died, acres of land went out of cultivation without the labour to tend them. The monasteries lost many of their brethren, parishes were without clergy, and as a result many men, who would otherwise have been rejected, were appointed to fill positions in Church and State.

Not much is known about the earliest outbreaks in Chichester. Records show that in 1563 the plague killed about a quarter of the city's population. The city escaped the devastating plague of 1603 that killed over 30,000 in London. In the outbreaks of 1607 and 1608 the death rate increased by three times the normal incidence. In the parish of St Andrew the registers show that, from one death in 1606, there was a rise to 24 in 1607 and to 36 in 1608. At that time it was decided to close the church

for six months and the churchwardens complained to the dean that Constantine Turton, their curate, did not take services for 22 weeks. During the same period the number of burials in the parish of St Pancras rose from 12 to 72 and in that of St Peter the Great from 20 to 88. The September Quarter sessions for 1608 were put back to 1609 because of the plague.

In 1665 the Great Plague, which was raging at the time in London, reached Chichester when a visitor from the capital is reputed to have introduced it. He stayed in an inn and was found dead by the innkeeper in the morning. When the cause of death was realised his body was buried in St Pancras churchyard the same night by torchlight. The mayor ordered the closing of the city gates and nobody was allowed to enter or leave. It is said that the people of Bosham brought food which was left outside the west gate and that the money to pay for it was dropped into buckets of water. Houses in which deaths had occurred were boarded up, the bodies of the dead were buried in lime pits. Many of these were found by workmen building the housing estate in fields by St James' Hospital.

St Richard of Chichester

Chichester's patron saint, St Richard de Wych was born in 1197 at Droitwich, Worcestershire. He came from a family of prosperous farmers. As a child Richard is said to have been noted for his studious and devout nature. Whilst in his teens, his education was interrupted by the death of his parents. When the farm, which was taken over by his elder brother, fell into debt, Richard left his studies to work as a labourer until the time when the business was again successful. He then made his share over to his brother and left to pursue his education.

Richard studied at Oxford and later at Paris and Bologna. He returned to Oxford as Chancellor of the University and in 1235 was appointed by Edmund Rich, the Archbishop of

This statue of Chichester's patron saint and former bishop, by Philip Jackson, was erected on the forecourt of the Cathedral in 2001.

Canterbury, later St Edmund, to become his chancellor.

On the death of Edmund, Richard entered the Dominican Monastery in Orleans where he was ordained. He returned as a priest in the Kent parish of Charing and was again chosen, this time by Archbishop Boniface, to become chancellor.

When the Bishop of Chichester, Ralph Neville died in 1245 the Chapter chose King Henry's favourite, Robert Passelew to succeed him. This had been done despite Passelew being unlearned and unsuitable for the post. The Archbishop summoned a synod of bishops who refused Passelew's election, recommending Richard in his place. Accordingly Richard was appointed and consecrated at Lyons by Pope Innocent IV.

The king did all in his power to make Richard's position untenable. His manors were confiscated and he received no income, depending entirely upon the charity of the religious community. He stayed with the village priest, Simon, at Tarring from where he travelled around the diocese building up a reputation for humility and kindness. Eventually, under threat of excommunication by the Pope, the king relented and restored Richard's palace and manors to him.

Richard died in Dover on 3 April 1253 having carried out a mission set him by the Pope to preach in churches and parishes all along the south coast urging support for the Crusades to the Holy Land.

At that time, to have the tomb of a saint was certain to attract pilgrims, and thus prosperity, to both Cathedral and city. It was therefore not surprising that both the Chapter and the Corporation recommended Richard as a candidate for canonisation. This is not to decry his worthiness for such promotion. To justify the submission, tales of miracles that occurred during his lifetime and of cases of healing occasioned by visiting his tomb would need to be provided, fortunately these soon came to light.

One legend is that, during a Mass, Richard had once dropped a full chalice which fell to the ground and not a drop of wine was spilt. Accordingly, most representations of the saint show him with a chalice at his feet.

Richard's status as a saint was confirmed by Pope Urban on 22 January 1262, less than nine years after his death. In 1276, in a ceremony attended by Edward I with Queen Eleanor, the Archbishop of Canterbury and nine other bishops, his body was transferred to a shrine built in the Cathedral behind the High Altar.

The shrine soon became a popular place of pilgrimage, so much so that in 1478 Bishop Storey issued a decree banning the carrying of wands by visitors, as they were being used as

A conjectural view of the Greyfriars monastery painted by Mike Codd. The chapel in the foreground is all that survives. (*CDM*)

weapons in the unseemly fights and scuffles that had broken out within Chichester Cathedral. In 1538 Henry VIII ordered through his Chancellor, Thomas Cromwell, that the shrine should be destroyed. Richard's remains were dispersed and the accumulated gold, silver and other precious ornaments left by pilgrims was taken in six coffers to London for Henry's use.

Today the area behind the High Altar is dignified by a fine tapestry, known as the Anglo-German Tapestry, which was dedicated in June 1985. Designed by Ursula Benker-Schirmer it was paid for partly by the Cathedral Friends but mainly by donation from churches, both Catholic and Lutheran, in Germany.

Monastic Chichester

It has been estimated that in the 13th century one man in 50, throughout the country, was a cleric of some sort. It is reasonable to suppose that in Chichester the proportion was probably higher. Certainly a feature of life in the city at that time was the presence of friars and monks from the Dominican and Franciscan monasteries. These orders had come to England from the Continent, setting up houses in towns throughout the country to carry out their work of preaching and educating the poor.

The Franciscan Monks, or Greyfriars as they were popularly known, came to Chichester in about 1230. At first they lived in a convent that was built in St Martin's Square. In 1253, when St Richard left 20 shillings and his psalter to the Friars Minor of Chichester there were 26 brethren living there. The land on which the Chichester Castle, demolished in 1217, had been situated was given to the friars by Henry III in 1269. Here they set about building their new monastery buildings.

There was a Dominican, or Blackfriars,

Archaeologists excavate the skeletons from the former burial ground of the Blackfriars monastery in East Street prior to the construction of Stocklund House in 1966.

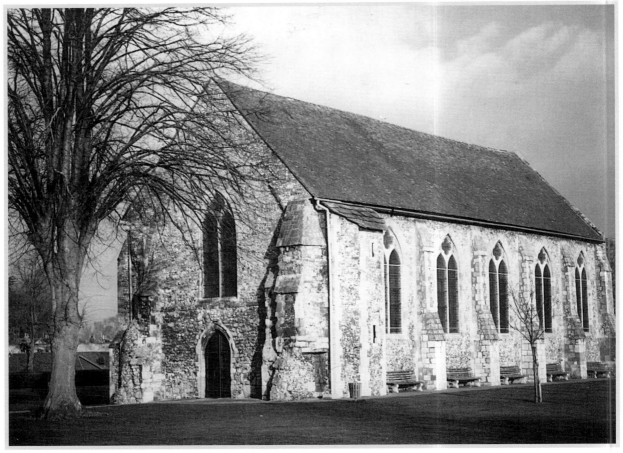

The former chapel to the Greyfriars monastery. The building has served as the city's guildhall, as the Assize Courthouse and as the militia drill room and rifle range. It is now used as an annexe to the Chichester District Museum.

Monastery in East Street on land where St John's Street is now situated. They had land given to them by Queen Eleanor in 1284 and again in 1286. The friars were apparently held in some esteem by the royal family of the time; when Edward I visited the city in 1297 and Edward II in 1324 they both gave sums of money to the 'Friar Preachers'

The monasteries survived until 1536 when Henry VIII's Suppression Act was passed by Parliament. It was introduced to correct many of the abuses of monasticism that Henry's Vicar-General, Thomas Cromwell found. He compiled a list of breaches of rules, of 'manifest sin' and other moral lapses, to justify the Act which transferred to the Crown the properties of

religious houses with an annual income of less than £200. There can be no doubt that the so-called reform had a profound effect upon life in Chichester.

The two Chichester friaries were both surrendered on 8 October 1538, their treasures were taken by the king and the monks pensioned or dispersed. In both establishments the number of brethren had been reduced over the years to seven. William Bradbridge, the mayor, accepted their goods on behalf of the king. The Blackfriars' site was sold to Edward Millet and the Greyfriars' chapel and grounds were given to the Corporation and the citizens of Chichester.

In 1966, when foundations were being dug for new shops and offices on the corner of St John's

Street and East Street, the Blackfriars' graveyard was uncovered and the skeletons of over 120 bodies unearthed.

All that now remains of the monastic presence in the city is the former Greyfriars' chapel in Priory Park. Over the succeeding centuries it has served as the city's guildhall, as a courthouse, as a base for the militia who set up a rifle range within it, and as a museum. It is still in use by the Chichester District Museum for some of their larger exhibits and visits can be arranged to view it.

The Bell Tower

Chichester Cathedral is the only English Cathedral to have its bells situated in a separate campanile, or bell tower. Several other

In this 1929 postcard picture of the Bell Tower the railings that enclosed the Cathedral churchyard can be seen.

cathedrals once had such structures which have not survived to the present day. The date of its construction is not clear, it is thought to have been about 1428 when former mayor, Thomas Patching, gave 100 marks towards its building.

The tower was formerly known as Ryman's, or Raymond's, Tower. There was a traditional local belief that the tower was built using stone that had been recovered from a man named Ryman. He had allegedly purchased the stone in order to build a castle but had been refused permission by Edward III. This legend probably originated from the fact that Ryman's house at Apuldram and the tower are built from similar Ventnor stone.

The tower contains a ring of eight bells, the earliest is dated 1583. The heaviest, weighing over a ton, was cast by Richard Phelps in 1706. The building also accommodates a clock which sounds the hours and quarters during daylight. The bells are rung every Sunday morning and to celebrate festivals or special occasions. In 1975 the Cathedral gift shop was opened in the basement.

A Chichester Tale – The Aerostatic Adventurer

This barely credible tale is about an event that took place in 1790. Strangely, there appears to have been no account of it published locally. This verbatim account is taken from the *Ipswich Journal* of 24 April that year.

"Mr Murray, who fome weeks fince defcended from Portfmouth church tower in a parachute, on Wednefday came down from the Bell tower of Chichefter Cathedral, but not with the fame fuccefs.

When about 14 feet from the top, a fudden guft of wind laid this bold aerostatic adventurer and the appuratus in a horizontal position: when on a level with the gutter of the Cathedral he righted, but an eddy of wind threw him a fecond time horizontally, in which fituation he fell to the ground with great force. The blood

This picture of a stonemason making repairs to the parapet of the Bell Tower, taken in 1963, gives some idea of the prospect that faced the intrepid Mr Murray when making his descent.

gufhed from his ears, nofe and mouth, moft plentifully; and he was carried to the Blue Anchor Inn without figns of life.

Four gentlemen of the faculty inftantly went to his affiftance; and in fomething more than four hours, animation returned, and in fix his fpeach was reftored. Mr Prefcot, one of the above gentleman, has conftantly attended him fince; and he is now out of danger."

Mr Prescott was a member of the staff of the Chichester Infirmary. Later in the same year it is told that the brave, but foolhardy, Mr Murray leapt from a church tower in Farnham.

Hospitals

The proliferation of nursing and rest homes in the later years of the 20th century had its counterpart in mediaeval times when most towns had hospitals to accommodate the needs of the old, the poor, the disabled and the sick. The administration of these hospitals, which were frequently charitable foundations, was usually the responsibility of a master and was conducted according to strict regulations, which among other matters governed the category of inmate to whom admission was afforded.

In 1158, Dean William had founded the Hospital of St Mary. This was originally sited on land now occupied by the Royal Arms Public

A 1907 postcard showing St Mary's Hospital and chapel.

A internal view of the hospital showing the construction of the mediaeval roof seen in the previous picture.

House in East Street. The hospital moved to its present site in St Martin's Square when it was vacated by the Franciscans in 1269. The hospital is thought to be the oldest foundation of its kind in the country still in use for its original purpose.

A mediaeval hospital building would most often comprise a chapel opening on to a hall which served as an infirmary ward. Although the building at St Mary's has been shortened these features can still be seen. The infirmary hall has been subdivided so that individual rooms are now where the beds used to stand. The magnificent timber roof is still a outstanding feature.

The number of inmates at St Mary's varied. We learn from a visitation carried out by Bishop Reade in 1402 that the 13 poor inmates were being defrauded of their daily ration of broth and weekly allowance of one groat. In 1478

there were, besides the warden, a chaplain and five residents.

At the time of the Reformation the control of St Mary's passed to the Cathedral's dean and chapter who are still responsible for it. Eight single persons and four married couples now live in the hospital and its associated cottages.

Of greater antiquity than St Mary's was St James' Hospital for lepers situated about a mile east of the city. An early deed shows that the hospital was in existence before the charter of Bishop Seffrid in 1180. This charter refers to the gift of 'eight cloth tunics and a bacon pig at Christmas to the leprous folk without the gates'. The hospital's master was paid two pence a day for carrying out his duties. The inmates were allowed to leave the house only to beg for alms, they were expelled if they were found to be married or even incontinent. The hospital appears to have been closed by 1618 and the

This cottage is all that remains of the former leper hospital which was destroyed by fire in 1782.

buildings were destroyed after a disastrous fire in 1781. All that remains on the site is a cottage that was built in the 18th century using materials salvaged from the ruined hospital. It stands in Westhampnett Road by the River Lavant and has a commemorative plaque on its front wall.

During the 12th and 13th centuries leprosy was a major disease throughout Europe and dealing with those infected was a constant problem. There are records of three other leper houses existing in the neighbourhood of Chichester. The hamlet of Maudlin, near Westhampnett, was so named from its association with the nearby hospital of St Mary Magdalen which was last mentioned in a bequest dated 1418. William of Kainesham (Kingsham) gave money to the Lepers of Whyke, probably the leper house that existed at Rumboldswyke. This establishment also benefited from the will of John, the Cathedral chancellor, in 1374; a similar institution is recorded at Stockbridge in the same document.

The City's Mediaeval Parishes

The City was first divided into parishes in mediaeval times, each having its own church and serving a population of 300–400 people. Although some of these parishes survived into the 20th century they have all now disappeared, having been amalgamated in 1952 by an order in council which joined the parishes and benefices of St Olave, St Martin, St Andrew, St Peter the Great, St Peter the Less and All Saints.

St Olave's Church can be seen in this picture taken just before its closure in 1956, it is now the SPCK bookshop.

St Peter the Less Church was built before 1350, it was demolished in April 1957 and the land sold to the Portsmouth Co-op Society to build their new store.

St Peter the Great became the parish church of the united parish.

The parish of St Peter the Great, was probably the oldest of the city's parishes having been based on the Saxon Minster. For many centuries it did not have its own church, services being conducted in the nave of the Cathedral. In 1852 it moved to the newly built church of St Peter the Great in West Street, also know as the subdeanery. This building is now in use as a public house having become redundant as a church when the parish was joined with that of St Paul in 1976.

The parish of St Olave had its church in North Street, the building being the smallest and oldest of the city's churches. The dedication to St Olave, or Olaf, who was King of Norway from 995 to 1030 and responsible for bringing Christianity to that country, must have been after his canonisation in 1164. This would indicate that the parish existed early in the 13th century. The nave however was built at least 100 years earlier and there is some evidence that a building dating back to Saxon times stood on the site. The parish, together with the other small parishes of

There are many of the original parish boundary stones still to be seen throughout the city. This one in Lion Street, dated 1709, marks the extent of the parish of St Olave.

the city, was amalgamated with that of St Peter the Great in 1956, and the church is now used as the SPCK bookshop.

Henry III gave permission in 1229 to pull down the parish church of St Peter in the Market and to transfer its two parishioners to St Mary's Hospital. This church was sited in East Street, approximately where the Royal Arms stands today. There is a reference in the 1402 records of St Mary's Hospital of the need to repair the chancel of 'St Mary in the Market'. It seems probable therefore that the church was not immediately demolished but used as a chapel for the inmates of the hospital.

The parish of St Andrew's Oxmarket extended from Hog Lane, now known as St Martin's Street, to Cow Lane, now vanished. As the names suggest this was the market area of the city and the most densely populated. The first naming of the church is in documents of 1248, and like other churches in the city it was apparently built on the site or an earlier chapel. Maybe because of its proximity to the market there seem to be many incidents of brawling in the churchyard recorded in the churchwardens accounts. Many at the city's foremost citizens lived in the parish including the Cawley Family, the Bullakers, who were a leading Catholic household, and the family of William Collins, the Chichester poet who was born in the parish in 1720. The church was damaged by German bombs during the raid on the city in February 1942 and it was never again used as a church. The building, which is approached from an alley to the north of East Street, now serves as Chichester's arts centre.

The Pallants in Chichester formed a part of the city which came under the jurisdiction of the Archbishop of Canterbury. Why and when this came about is not known, but it was certainly so at the time of the Domesday Book. The church of All Saints in West Pallant, now the local headquarters of the Red Cross, is the only church in Chichester shown in that record. The structure

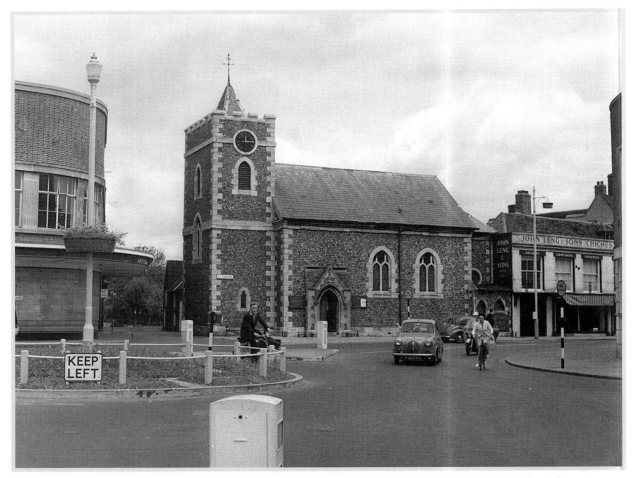

The original church of St Pancras was a 13th-century structure. It was destroyed in the Civil War and the present church built on the site in 1750.

is contemporary with St Andrew's and St Olave's dating from the early 13th century.

There are records that, at one time, other churches existed within the walls. St Martin's was taken down in 1906, the church's bell, which was installed in 1405, was removed to the Church of St Mary in Rumboldswyke; in 2001 it was transferred to St Wilfrid's Church in Sherborne Road. St Peter the Less in North Street survived until 1956, its presence is perpetuated in the name of the street that has been formed on its former site.

We know little about the parishes of St Peter sub Castro, St Andrews in the Pallant and Our Lady upon Northgate other than brief references in contemporary documents.

Outside the walls, by the east gate, is the church and parish of St Pancras. The first known reference to the church is found in the 1291 taxation accounts of Pope Nicholas. There are few records, other than the names of some of its priests, until the 16th century when the church seems to have been known for its puritan preaching which attracted many Non-Conformist worshippers. This led to complaints from the other clergy in the city and discontent among the parishioners who often could not find even standing room at services. In 1635 William Speed, the rector, was admonished for being 'popular in the pulpit' and made to pull down a gallery he had built in the church to cater for the additional congregation.

Tucked away in Mount Lane off Westgate, the former parish church of St Bartholomew is unknown to many of the city's residents. It was built in 1832. Today it is the chapel to the religious community of the Servants of the Cross.

During the siege of the city in 1642, the church was used to mount a cannon and, in the ensuing fighting, the building was destroyed. It remained in a ruined state until 1750 when it was rebuilt, apparently on its original foundations.

The parish was one of the most populated in the 19th century and in 1868 the church was enlarged.

Also destroyed in the Civil War was the parish church of St Bartholomew, outside the west gate. Like St Pancras church it also served a small community living outside of the city walls. The church seems to have had a dual dedication for it was also known as St Sepulchre's. Both names appeared in records for the parish dating to the early 15th century.

The church had been built as a round church in the manner of the church of the Holy Sepulchre in Jerusalem, leading to its alternative name. The present building was constructed in 1832 but the parish is now amalgamated with that of St Peter and St Paul. The church served as the chapel for the Chichester Theological College until that establishment closed, and it is, at the time of writing, disused.

The Streets

In mediaeval times it was the responsibility of householders to keep the street in front of their property paved and clean, they also were required to hang out a lamp over their doorway and take their turn in keeping a watch at night.

This arrangement was apparently unsatisfactory as, during the reign of Elizabeth I when the city Corporation found it necessary to obtain an Act of Parliament to pave the main streets, the preamble to the Act reported the streets as being 'very mierie, and full of waterie and durtie places, both lothsome and noysome' The areas paved by the Corporation included the market places and 'other places of greatest repayre, whereby the people of the sayde Citie and Countrey neare adioyning have received great pleasure and ease'.

Following a further Act in 1575 the responsibility was returned to the landowners who were required, if ordered by the mayor, to pave their frontages up to the channel in the middle of the street. They could be subject to a fine of 3s 4d (18p) for every square yard unpaved within two months.

The Act was administered by the Court Leet. The court records before 1685 have not survived, but from that date there are references to many householders being brought before the court for such offences as uncleaned gutters, encroachments, dunghills, etc.

In 1753 when the Board of Guardians of the Poor was set up, in addition to their other obligations, they were given the responsibility of providing lamps and 'enlightening the streets' of the city.

They were authorised to collect a lamp rate for so doing. The guardians' minute books show that there were 100 oil lamps provided, which were maintained and lit by a lamplighter who in 1770 was paid £2.16s (£2.80) 'per moon' (presumably every lunar month of 28 days). It appears that the Board had trouble from dishonest

This conjectural view of East Street in the early 16th century was created by artist Mike Codd. (*CDM*)

A fine picture of the Cross taken in about 1900. Note the delivery of ale being made to the Anchor Inn on the left of the scene.

lamplighters, one of them, James Roberts, embezzled 118 gallons of oil.

The Market Cross

The Market Cross, situated at the crossing of the city's four main streets, is Chichester's centrepiece and best-known landmark. Although not unique it is generally recognised as the finest structure of its kind the country and was given to the citizens by Bishop Edward Storey in 1501. The bishop was concerned to see traders selling their goods in the open in all weathers. His gift was to be for 'the sucoure and comfort of the poore peple to sell their chafer there' which privilege was to be free from local taxes.

The Cross has undergone many changes over the centuries and has been in constant need of repair and restoration. Originally it was topped by a grand finial with niches containing statues of saints. This was removed in 1724, to be

This bust of Charles I was made for the king by Le Sueur in the 1630s. How it came into the possession of the City Council who placed it in the central niche of the Cross in about 1580 is not clear. When its value was realised in 1978 a fibreglass replica was made to replace it, the original is now kept in the Pallant House Gallery. (CCC)

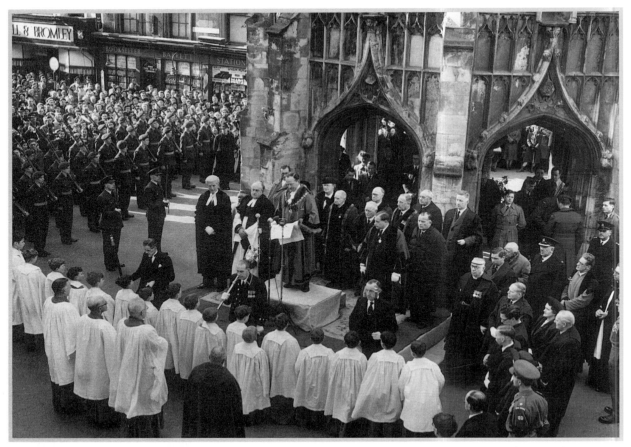

For 500 years the Cross has been the traditional spot for issuing public announcements. On 8 February 1952 the mayor, George Russell Purchase, proclaimed the accession of Her Majesty Queen Elizabeth II.

replaced with a clock and bell presented by Lady Farrington in memory of her husband. The present cupola was installed in place of the clock in 1745 when the clock faces were added and paid for by the 2nd Duke of Richmond. A bust of Charles I can be seen in a recess on the east face of the Cross, which is a modern copy of the bronze bust installed in the 17th century to replace an earlier likeness of Bishop Storey.

The Cross has long been the recognised site for public proclamations. In 1642, during the Civil War, the mayor, Robert Exton, read a communication from the king which was to have significant consequences for him, as will be noted in a later chapter. In the 17th century the town crier would announce the Mayor's Court from the Cross and in the 20th century the death

of monarchs and the accession of the new sovereign has been proclaimed there by the mayor.

When the Corporation opened the North Street Market House in 1808 many traders preferred to continue to deal from the Cross rather than pay the new market's tolls. The Corporation responded by closing the arches in the Cross with railings. These remained until 1872 when the Council removed them at a cost of £82 14s (£82.70), the original cost of the railings 64 years earlier had been £64.8s (£64.40).

The 500th anniversary of the Market Cross was celebrated in 2001. The original ceremony was re-enacted with the present bishop, the Right Reverend John Hind, and the mayor, Michael Shone, taking part.

This 1920s view of West Street shows the Prebendal School on the right. The 13th-century building was rebuilt in 1830.

The Prebendal School

In addition to his gift of the Market Cross, the citizens of Chichester have another reason to be grateful to Bishop Storey. In 1497 he refounded the former Cathedral song school and endowed to it the income of the Prebend of Highleigh. It is known from statutes that the original school was in existence as long ago as 1232 and it is quite possible that, in common with most Norman cathedrals, it was created when the See was removed from Selsey in 1075.

The school was housed in the schoolroom in West Street that still forms part of its premises. Pupils were divided into two categories, the scholars who were fee-paying pupils, and the choristers who were paid for by the Cathedral authorities in return for their services in the choir.

In the 16th century there were usually about 12 choristers who were tutored in singing by the Precentor. The education that they obtained necessarily suffered as a result of their commit-

ments to the choir. The scholars received a basic schooling in grammar, Latin and logic and they paid a fee of about half a crown (12½p) per annum with a further shilling (5p) a week for their keep should they be boarders.

Many former pupils of the school have gone on to achieve national fame. Among these 'prebendalians' were William Juxon, who became Archbishop of Canterbury, Chichester MP William Cawley (more is written about these two individuals in a later chapter), John Selden the distinguished 17th-century lawyer and the poet James Hurdis.

In 1784 the headmaster, the Revd David Davies, Doctor of Divinity, invited pupils to the school 'where young Gentlemen are duly instructed in the Classics, or in any other part of the School learning agreeable to their intended Appointments in Life' The cost of tuition was four guineas (£4.20p) a year for day boys and 20 guineas (£21) for boarders.

The Cathedral choristers at rehearsal under the tuition of the Master of Choristers in the former chapter house, which is used for their practice room. (*Hugh Curtis*)

Today the school is the oldest school in Sussex, the 13th-century schoolhouse, with its long dormitory on the upper floor is still in use, although the school has expanded to take in adjoining properties and part of the east wing of the Bishop's Palace. It maintains its links with the Cathedral and still provides its choristers. Since 1972, when girls were first admitted, it has been a co-educational preparatory school with day and boarding pupils.

The Cathedral choir process through the Cloisters on Palm Sunday 2002. (*Hugh Curtis*)

THE LATER MIDDLE AGES

The City in 1600

IN THE early years of the 17th century the population numbered about 2,500, most of whom lived within the walls or in the poorer extra-mural suburbs of St Pancras and St Bartholomew. The wealthier professionals and tradespeople dwelt in large timber-framed houses along the main streets. The north-western sector contained gardens and orchards. Markets were held twice a week in the open area surrounding the Market Cross. The Pallant area was the centre of the brewing, leather-working and tanning industries.

The city was governed by the city Corporation, an elected body comprising a mayor, aldermen, and the free citizens of the city. Meetings were held in the Town Hall, a building sited in the centre of North Street. The right of taking part in the election of the mayor and two members representing the city in Parliament was shared by the common members of the Merchants' Guild and the commoners of

This 1610 map by John Speed shows how little development had taken place outside the city walls. This situation had changed little by the time of the siege of the city in 1642. Note the Guildhall set in the centre of North Street.

Canon Gate in South Street was erected in the 16th century to preserve the privacy of the Cathedral precincts. It contained a porter's lodge on the upper floor. The coat of arms above the arch are those of Bishop Sherburne.

the city. The latter met and voted at the Guildhall, the former chapel of the Franciscan monastery that had passed to the city corporation on the dissolution of that establishment in 1541.

Chichester sent two members to the House of Commons. It was the practice for the Guild to select one member and the commoners the other, however it was necessary for the commoners' member to be nominated by the Guild. This procedure was completely unconstitutional and was not to the commoners liking, as it effectively gave the Guild the right to veto their choice. The Guild's member was most often the city's recorder.

Needlemaking

The Chichester needlemaking industry has appeared large in published histories of the city, whose importance as the national centre for the manufacture of needles is well established. Yet Roy Morgan, in his book *Chichester, a Documentary History*, has pointed out that, in terms of the total economy of the town, it was nowhere near as vital as wool, grain, or cattle. It was mainly carried out in St Pancras, its existence being recorded as early as 1308. By 1600 almost every house in St Pancras was occupied by a needlemaker.

The destruction of part of the suburb during the Civil War, combined with competition from cheaper Midland manufacturing methods, led to a decline in local needlemaking after 1650, although needle-makers are recorded as living in St Pancras until 1788. An idea of the prosperity of those engaged in the trade is given by the inventory dated 1733 of Isaac Hammond, who lived on the River Lavant's bank in St Pancras. The rooms in his property included a kitchen, pantry, brewhouse and parlour with two bed-chambers over. Stock included 12,500 quilting needles, 31,000 happles, 36,000 square needles and 12,000 glover's needles, with a total value of £92. The house and garden were mortgaged, with £205 outstanding.

Needlemaking was a cottage industry, obtaining its supplies of iron from the Weald. Availability of a water supply from the Lavant might have helped to decide the siting. The workers did not aspire to guild status, possibly because they were one industry which did not feel threatened by local competition.

The Civil War

The Civil War commenced when Charles I raised his standard at Nottingham on 22 August 1642. In Sussex the population was evenly split between the two factions, even the 28 Members of Parliament for the various county constituencies were divided, with 17 members supporting the Parliamentarians, or Roundheads and 11 the Royalists, or Cavaliers.

Within Chichester, most of the Cathedral clergy and some of the local gentry were for the king's cause, with the city's merchants and the majority of the residents taking the side of the Parliamentary forces. The two Members of Parliament, Christopher Lewkenor, the city's Recorder, and Sir William Morley of Halnaker, were both Royalists. The leading local Parliamentarian was William Cawley, the Chichester brewer, who had formerly been the member for Chichester but at the time of the war represented Midhurst.

In June an order was issued by Parliament instructing the militia in each county to secure the possession of the magazines of arms and ammunition The king replied by issuing a proclamation countermanding the order. The mayor,

The city walls and Cathedral from the Westgate Fields in 1961. A view that was virtually unchanged from that which greeted Waller's besieging troops in 1642.

Robert Exton, having read the proclamation at the Cross, fled to York to join the king rather than face the wrath of the Parliamentarians

On 24 August, William Cawley declared the city to be for Parliament. The Cathedral clergy replied by raising a body of light horse in support of the royal cause and drilling in the Cathedral Close. Local Royalists received a setback when Portsmouth fell to Parliamentary troops on 4 September. They countered on 15 November when, under the leadership of Sir William Morley, they forced the mayor to give up the city's keys and seized the magazine together with the guns. As Captain Chittey, the leader of the Militia, fled to Portsmouth, Sir Edward Ford, the High Sheriff of Sussex, marched into the city with a Royalist force that he had raised from various parts of the county.

Meanwhile a large Parliamentary army led by Sir William Waller had captured Winchester and started towards Chichester. Part of the force went to capture Arundel, which was taken quite easily and provided the attacking force with over 100 horses and a hoard of arms and stores.

Waller arrived outside Chichester's walls on 21 December 1642. His force numbered 6,000 men, having been joined by companies of Dragoons under Colonel Morley. A Royalist sortie from the city was repelled, with one man killed and another taken prisoner. Waller set up camp to the north of the city on the Broyle where, although under fire from the city's defenders, he managed to position a battery of guns. The following day he called upon the Royalists to surrender, when his demands were refused a bombardment of the city commenced. Much of this is recorded as having overshot the city. The next day he brought his gunners nearer to the walls, the defenders replied by deliberately setting fire to houses in the St Pancras and Westgate suburbs.

Waller's men managed to mount a cannon on the roof of St Pancras Church. From this position they could fire into the city, and also prevent the Royalist soldiers from showing themselves on the city walls. More Parliamentary troops from Arundel arrived on the sixth day of the siege. Under the command of Colonel Roberts, they took up positions outside the south gate.

Waller next prepared to petard the gate that led through the walls into the deanery gardens, as a precursor to making simultaneous attacks from the east and west. That evening a petition from the city requested a meeting at nine the next day, when surrender on Waller's terms was agreed.

Some 800 or so prisoners were taken, their leaders being conveyed, together with 50 officers, to London by sea. The events of the next few days are among the most dismal in the city's history. Waller's men went on to plunder the Cathedral. We have a graphic first-hand account of the action written by the Dean, Dr Bruno Reeves. He relates how the men led by Sir Arthur Haselrig seized the Cathedral's ornaments, including the communion plate from the altar. They smashed the communion table and the organs, prayer books and vestments were torn and thrown about the building. They ran up and down the building with their swords in their hands hacking at the seats and stalls and defacing pictures and monuments. A member of the Cathedral Chapter revealed that much of the Cathedral's plate was hidden in a secret room behind panelling in the Chapter House. Reeves tells of the delight shown by Haselrig as the panelling was smashed to gain access and the plate stolen.

The Parliamentary troops remained garrisoned at Chichester for four years until March 1646 when they left the citizens to rebuild their city. Those who had led the Royalists in the city were punished. Sir Edward Ford was sent to London but was soon released and within the year he was again leading troops for the king. Most of the others were fined, the clergy were deprived of their income, Dean Reeves was fined £120.

Bishop King was stripped of his position, which he resumed after the Restoration.

William Cawley

Chichester abounds with many buildings of architectural merit and historic interest. A gem among these, that is maybe not as well appreciated as it should be, is the chapel of St Bartholomew's Hospital in Broyle Road.

The hospital was founded in 1626 by William Cawley, probably to meet the wishes of his father who died in 1621. His intention being an almshouse for the 'residence and maintenance of 12 decayed tradesmen of Chichester'. In 1681 the building became the property of the city Corporation who ran it as an almshouse for the poor of the city until 1753, when an Act of Parliament converted it into the city's workhouse.

William Cawley was born in Chichester in 1602, the son of John Cawley, a wealthy brewer who had been three times mayor of the city. William must have been a man of remarkable ability, he was first educated in Chichester, at the Prebendal School. He graduated from Hart Hall in 1621 and in 1627 was elected as the Member of Parliament for Midhurst at the age of 25.

In 1628 Cawley was elected as MP for Chichester, His early years in Parliament were without much distinction, except maybe when, in 1628, he and the city's other MP, Henry Bellingham, were summoned to Westminster answer for the refusal of the citizens of Chichester to billet two companies of troops prior to their sailing to France. On arrival in London they were both released.

In 1640 Cawley was re-elected to the so-called Long Parliament which sat until 1653. He was also chosen in both 1647 and 1659. In Westminster he became one of the followers of Oliver Cromwell's Parliamentary Party, or Roundheads as they became known.

The central structure is the chapel to William Cawley's almshouses, subsequently the Chichester workhouse.

A portrait of William Cawley the founder of St Bartholomew's Hospital.

With the outbreak of the Civil War Cawley was commissioned into the Parliamentary Army. He was active in Chichester and, when the Royalists seized the city, he fled to Portsmouth. It was as a result of the letter that he wrote to the Speaker, Mr Lenthall, to inform him of the Royalist's coup that Sir William Waller's force set off into Sussex and recaptured Chichester.

After the war, Cawley was appointed one of the Commissioners for Sussex. His work included investigating the County's clergy, many of whom were suspected of having Royalist sympathies. Cawley took his duties seriously, personally attending the ejection of Samuel Hill from his Church at Boxgrove. Locally he served as a JP on the Chichester Bench and as a churchwarden of the parish of Rumboldswyke.

About this time he acquired the property in South Pallant known as Cawley Priory, which had been forfeited by the Bowyer family of Rumboldswyke for supporting the Royalist cause.

In 1649 Cawley was one of the 131 persons nominated to sit as the High Court of Justice to try Charles I for treason. Of those judges only 59, of whom Cawley was one, chose to sign the king's death warrant.

When the monarchy was restored in 1660 Cawley fled the country and settled first in Belgium and later in the Swiss town of Vevay, where he lived out his days. He died there in 1666 and for many years it was thought that he was buried there.

However, it appears that in his old age, Cawley had often yearned to be in the city of his birth, and it was always his wish to be buried in the chapel of the almshouses he had founded so many years before. There is no doubt that feeling against the regicides, as those who had authorised Charles's execution were known, was so strong that there was no question of even his body being allowed back into the country.

In 1816, when workmen were repairing the floor of the chapel, a vault was discovered, in which were two coffins and one body wrapped in an envelope of lead. It was almost certainly Cawley whose body had been smuggled into the country and secretly buried in accordance with his wishes. Today a small stone plaque marks the spot in the chapel where his remains have been reinterred.

Cawley's son John became the Rector of Rotherfield in 1658 and, after the Restoration, he disowned the beliefs and actions of his father. He was appointed Archdeacon of Lincoln Cathedral in 1666.

William Juxon

A Chichester-born contemporary of Cawley was William Juxon. Although they were on opposing sides in the Civil War, they were both former pupils of the Prebendal School. One feels that they must have met at some time, although no record of such a meeting is known.

William Juxon was born in the city in 1582 where his father, Richard, was a lawyer and a

William Cawley's own pew, complete with carved initials, was allowed to stay in the chapel despite his being condemned for signing the King's death warrent.

Cathedral official. William was baptised in the parish of St Peter the Great, which at that time was sited within the Cathedral's north transept. The font in which the ceremony was carried out is still in use today in St Paul's Church.

Juxon was educated at the Merchant Tailors' School and at St John's College Oxford. He rose quickly through the ranks of the church serving as Dean of Worcester and Bishop of Hereford, before becoming Bishop of London in 1633 as well as the chaplain to Charles I. It was in this capacity that he attended the fated king on the scaffold at his execution.

During the period in which the country was governed by the Parliamentarians, Juxon retired to Albourne Place in Gloucestershire. There is a story that one day Government troops were seen

approaching to take the bishop prisoner. He quickly grabbed a hod of mortar and climbed a ladder to join the masons who were conveniently at that time repairing the roof, and thus escaped arrest.

Chichester-born William Juxon, Archbishop of Canterbury, and chaplain to Charles I, on the scaffold at his execution.

On the Restoration, Juxon was created Archbishop of Canterbury and it was he who officiated at the coronation of Charles II in 1660, having the honour of placing the crown upon the king's head. He was an old man on his appointment and only held on to the archiepiscopal seat for three years until his death in 1663, aged 80.

In common with Cawley, William Juxon never forgot the city of his birth and in his will left £100 to the poor people of the Parish of St Peter the Great. His name was not commemorated in Chichester until the 1970s when a small development of houses off Stirling Road was named Juxon Close, a narrow footpath connecting it to Cawley Road.

1700–1800

THE 18th century has been described as Chichester's golden age. During the period it consolidated its position as the local centre of trade and of civil and legal administration. It was, of course, already the seat of the bishop and therefore the centre of the diocesan management of Sussex. Professional and businessmen prospered, there was an increase in house building, both within the Walls and in the surrounding villages, many of the fine brick-fronted houses with their elegant doorways that are a feature of the city were built at this time.

Spershott's Memoirs

We are fortunate that we have James Spershott's record of events within the city during his lifetime. His memoirs chronicle many changes and provide us with a unique insight into life in 18th-century Chichester.

Spershott was born at Shopwyke in 1710. In 1734 he married Martha Smith, who was the daughter of John Smith, the younger of the Smith brothers, the Chichester artists. James died in 1789 and was buried in St Pancras churchyard, as was Martha who had pre-deceased him in 1775.

Spershott trained as a joiner. He had long been a member of the Eastgate Baptist Chapel when, in 1756, he was ordained as its pastor. In his old age he wrote a history of England for his own satisfaction and, to save his childrens' children from expending time or expense in books, to this document he attached his own personal memoirs of Chichester.

He remembered that in his young days the city had been in a state of some decay, the streets were not paved, much of the damage caused in

The White Horse: The inn is known to have been in existence in 1604. The Georgian brick front covers a timber-framed building.

the Civil War had not been made good and the walls were in a ruinous state. The houses were 'in general very low, very old, and had their fronts framed with timber which lay bare to the weather'. Most buildings had a step down from the street to the ground floor with the first floors projecting out over the pavement.

In the city's main streets the shops had shutters to their fronts, which were taken down during the daytime leaving the premises quite open to the street. He could remember few houses at that time that were fronted with bricks,

More popularly known as the Old Punch House, the Royal Arms Inn, shown here in this 1960 photograph, was formerly the town house of the Lumley family. Spershott remembered the building being 'put to the modern taste'.

and those that were had been done recently. As a joiner he noted that, in the main streets, only about eight houses had sash windows, the others had transome windows with the glass set in lead. The former house of the Lumley family, now the Royal Arms, in East Street had been 'put to the modern taste' the former frontage having been clad in oak, blackened with age.

Little London, which Spershott describes as being 'now so gay', had contained 'only a few old houses, the street not pitched but very dirty with deep cart ruts'. The road from the north gate to the Broyle was 'deep, dirty, narrow and crooked'

Memories of the city's inhabitants were not favourable, Spershott thought that the city Corporation were a respectable body, however he describes drinking as being the 'reigning vice' with 'great drinkers among all ranks of men' There had been 45 public houses within the city. Farmers would come to market and get drunk, staying two or three days before their wives came to fetch them.

In his younger years he remembered there being many corpulent men and women in the city, some 'so fatted that they could hardly move about'. Among the recreations enjoyed by the citizens were bull-baiting, wrestling, cudgeling and footballing in the streets 'to the advantage of the glazier', there was also cock-fighting, dog-fighting and badger-baiting.

The memoirs relate that most families made their own bread, spun their own cloth and made their own household physic or herbal remedies. Their bacon racks, he said, were loaded with bacon. Spershott concluded by noting that during his lifetime he had seen 'almost the whole city rebuilt or refaced, as if another Cissa (see page 24) had been here'.

A Warning to Swearers

James Spershott was not one to miss an opportunity to make a moral point. An example

in his memoirs is his account of the sad story of Robert Madlock. It is recounted here in his words.

'Robert Madlock, a most profane swearer, being employed in the cleaning of the outside of the steeple, as he hung from a rope in his cradle from the walks on the west side, the rope broke and he fell upon the roof of the church and from thence to the parapet wall where he lye for some time crying and roaring most grievously, which I heard, and also saw let him down with a tackle in a coffin which happened to be ready made. When he came down he was scarce alive and expired soon after. A warning to swearers.'

The City Rebuilt

As Spershott recorded, many old timber-framed buildings had their fronts renewed or were re faced in brickwork. New building also proceeded at some pace during the period. Notable among the new houses was John Edes' house in West Street and Pallant House, built in 1712 by Henry 'Lisbon' Peckham, a wealthy merchant.

In 1731 the city corporation built the Council House in North Street to replace the old Council

The Council Chamber in the Council House is arguably the most elegant room in the city, its walls are lined with boards listing previous mayors. (CCC)

A 1960 picture of the fine house, built in 1696 by John and Hannah Edes. It became known as Wren House following an incorrect attribution to Sir Christopher Wren. It was purchased by the County Council in 1916 and used as offices until the construction of the County Hall in its grounds.

Chamber that stood in the centre of North Street. They chose as their architect Roger Morris, one of the leading exponents of the Palladian style. This choice may have been a measure of the growing influence of the Duke of Richmond in local affairs. Morris was, at the time, carrying out work for the duke at Goodwood. In 1783 the Assembly Rooms were added to the Council House to the design of James Wyatt.

Two Non-Conformist chapels, Baffin's Hall built in 1721 and Providence Chapel built in Chapel Street in 1809 still survive.

Built in 1731 to the design of Roger Morris, the Council House replaced the former Guildhall that stood in the centre of North Street.

A drawing by S.H. Grimm depicting the east gate, seen from inside the city just before its demolition in 1783. A Swiss artist, Grimm settled in England in 1769. Much of his work featured the Sussex landscape.

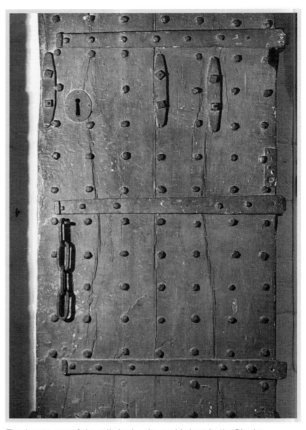

The door to one of the cells in the city gaol is kept in the District Museum, the names of some of those detained there are to be seen scratched on it. (*Keith Smith*)

A 1920 postcard showing the former gaol on the right.

The north, west and south gates of the city were taken down in 1773 but, because the city gaol was housed in its upper storey, the east gate remained until 1783. The new prison building was sited on the south side of East Street, immediately adjacent to the old gate.

The first prisoner held in the prison is recorded as being a young maidservant to Lady Franklin who had stolen some towels from her employer. Although pregnant she was sentenced to seven years transportation. The cell in which she was held was cold, with a stone floor and the walls running with water. Her distraught husband was not allowed to see her. She was taken to a prison ship in the Thames where she died awaiting the journey. The new building was demolished in 1935, having become the city's police station in 1836.

Oliver Whitby School

In 1702 Oliver Whitby, a Cicestrian and the son of Archdeacon Whitby, died aged 38. In his will he left property to endow a school for '12 poor boys' from Chichester, Harting or West Wittering. In addition to reading, writing and arithmetic the pupils were to be instructed 'with particular regard to navigation' The school opened in 1712, and at its peak in 1876 it provided an education for 52 boys.

The boys became a familiar feature in the city with their distinctive long blue coats, cap and yellow stockings leading to the popular name for the school of 'the Blue Coats'. The school, which was situated in West Street, was rebuilt in 1904, and survived until 1950. When it closed, its assets were used to provide scholarships for boys to attend Christ's Hospital School. The façade of the school building is preserved in the Army and Navy Store.

Two 18th-Century Personalities

The social life of the city in the 18th century was dominated by a few wealthy families. Among them was that of William Collins, a tradesman

The Army Navy store was once the home of the Oliver Whitby School, built in 1904. It replaced the earlier school building of the school founded in 1702.

Widely admired as one of the city's finest buildings, Lisbon Peckham's house at the crossing of the Pallants is now the Pallant House Gallery. (*Anne Scicluna*)

who was three times the city's mayor. The site of his house in East Street is now occupied by the Halifax Building Society. His son, also named William, born in 1721, is remembered as Chichester's poet. The younger Collins was among the earliest pupils at the Oliver Whitby School. He went on to study at Winchester and then Oxford, where he published the first of his writings. A man of great scholarship, he seems to have been of an indolent disposition which made him unsuitable for employment. He lived on the proceeds of property left him by his mother. Although his 'Odes' were well received he received little financial reward for his work. His health declined and in June 1759 he died in poverty at the age of 38. He was buried in St Andrew's Church adjacent to his birthplace. There is a fine memorial to him in the Cathedral by Flaxman which refers to his 'rays of genius'.

Henry Peckham is remembered as the Chichester merchant for whom Pallant House was built. He was known by the name of 'Lisbon' Peckham which has been thought to refer to his activities as an importer of wine from the Portuguese capital. His grandfather, Sir Henry Peckham had been a distinguished lawyer and politician who had served as Chichester's Recorder and MP. His son John, Lisbon's father, had been a spendthrift who frittered away his inheritance and, after his death in 1700 left his wife destitute, having mortgaged South Mundham Farm which had been her property.

Henry's early career is unclear. He was successful enough to repay his father's debts and by 1711 he had taken back the control of South Mundham Farm. That same year, at the age of 27, he married Elizabeth Albery, a wealthy 40-year-old widow. They commissioned the building of Pallant House soon after their marriage and were in residence by June 1713.

The marriage did not survive for long, by 1716 they separated and faced each other in court. Elizabeth claimed that Henry had converted most of her £10,000 fortune to his own uses. The case lingered on for four years and ended with Henry having to pay his wife the £50 a year 'pin money' promised her at the time of their marriage and a settlement of £3,500.

Peckham continued to live in Pallant House until at least 1740. He took part in local politics but never achieved his ambition of becoming the city's mayor. He died, aged 80, in 1764 and was buried in All Saints' Church in West Pallant. Today Pallant House is an art gallery containing one of the finest collections of British 20th-century art in the country.

The Dukes of Richmond

No history of Chichester would be complete without some mention of the Dukes of Richmond and the contribution that they have made to that history.

Their biographies have been recorded in other publications, the following sections concentrate on their association with the city.

The 1st Duke was born on 29 July 1672, the son of Charles II. His mother, Louise de Kéroualle, is said to have been a favourite among the Sovereign's mistresses. The king's marriage to Queen Catherine produced no heir; however his many liaisons with ladies of the court were more fruitful and at least 12 of his children are known to have survived, five of his sons were given dukedoms.

Before his first birthday the young Charles, Louise's son, was made Duke of Richmond, Earl of March and Baron of Settrington. In 1675 he was given the further titles of Duke of Lennox, Earl of Darnley and Baron of Torbolton. The duke spent much of his childhood with his mother in France where he was brought up as a

St James' Pillar. The obelisk was presented to the city by the 2nd Duke of Richmond to mark his serving as mayor in 1735. It was overturned by vandals soon after, following a rumour that a gold sovereign had been placed under it.

Catholic. He served in the French army and fought against the British in Flanders.

In 1692 he returned to England and changed his religious beliefs to become a Protestant. He appears to have devoted most of his days to hunting, gambling and drinking. To follow the celebrated Charlton Hunt he bought a 200-acre estate at Goodwood with a mansion house that he used as a hunting lodge. The property became a favourite residence and it was here, in 1701, that his first son was born. As with all of the subsequent elder sons of the Dukes of Richmond he was named Charles and given the title of the Earl of March.

A story is told that the 2nd Duke's marriage to Lady Sarah Cadogan was arranged by his father to settle a gambling debt to her father, Lord Cadogan. The bride was just 13 years old and her husband 18. He left to travel on the Continent immediately after the ceremony, the bride remaining with her parents. On his return three years later he was at the theatre when he noticed a beautiful young woman. Asking who she was, he was told that she was Lady March, his wife. Despite this unpromising start they became a devoted couple having a total of 12 children.

The 2nd Duke held many important State offices and, as Colonel of the Royal Horse Guards, fought at the Battle of Dettingen. Locally he was elected as a Member of Parliament for Chichester. This position was short-lived when he succeeded to the dukedom on the death of his father in May 1723. He took a keen interest in local affairs and he was the largest contributor to the fund for building the new Council House in North Street. The duke served as mayor in 1735 and he paid for the erection of the obelisk known

as St James Pillar to mark the eastern boundary of the city. He also undertook the 1756 restoration of the Cross at his own expense including a new clock and dials. On the local bench he was active in the pursuit of smugglers. He had plans to rebuild Goodwood House but was prevented by lack of funds, although by the time of his death in 1750 the estate had been enlarged to over 1,000 acres.

Of the 2nd Duke's 12 children, only seven survived into their teens. On his death in 1750, the title passed to his seventh child who was only 15 years old, two older sons having died in infancy. The 3rd Duke was a soldier like his father. He rose to the rank of major-general, commanding two regiments, and in 1765 he became ambassador to France. Whilst in France he acquired the collection of Sevrés porcelain that is still said to one of the finest in existence.

The 3rd Duke purchased land to increase the extent of the Goodwood Estate by 16,000 acres,

Goodwood House, rebuilt in 1783 by the 3rd Duke to the designs of Roger Morris. (*Goodwood Estate*)

Members of the corporation leave the Unicorn Inn on their way to Dear's almshouses with Christmas dinners for the residents, 1902.

he rebuilt Goodwood House enlarging the original building to form the Goodwood House that exists today.

St Pancras Corporation

Chichester possesses what, according to the *Guinness Book of Records*, is the oldest dining club in the world. The Ancient Corporation of St Pancras is a mock corporation that over three centuries has three times changed its constitution and aims.

The corporation was originally a political foundation, an Orange club pledging itself to William III. It was founded at the Unicorn Inn in Eastgate Square in 1689, The 1st Duke of Richmond, a cousin of William, sent 'a fatte bucke' to the inaugaral dinner on 4 November. The association of dukes with the Corporation has continued, the present duke was mayor in 1999 and 2000.

The original constitution included a mayor, aldermen, a town crier and common councillors. Since the Jacobite Rebellion of 1745 the political and religious bias has disappeared. The corporation became a club in which the prosperous professional men, the shopkeepers and tradesmen of the city met to dine in convivial surroundings and company. Tradition has it the Corporation received its nickname of 'the Wheelbarrow Club' from the apprentices who were instructed to wait outside the Unicorn with wheelbarrows to push their drunken masters home.

After some criticism of the Corporation's activities in the *Chichester Observer* it was decided in 1897 that it should supplement the income of the ladies in the dears almshouses in the Hornet, and also to provide them with a Christmas dinner every year.

In 1971 the old almshouses were sold and the

The burgesses of St Pancras Corporation in 1998 returning from their annual visit to the ladies of the Dear's charity. In accordance with tradition the city (uptown) mayor is pushed in a wheelbarrow followed by the St Pancras (downtown) mayor who was that year accompanied by the Duke of Richmond. The sharp-eyed reader might spot the author in this picture.

proceeds used to build four bungalows in St Pancras for elderly ladies. The corporation is now a registered charity with the aim of supporting the ladies and of building more houses for deserving ladies. Since the closure of the Unicorn in 1960, the Corporation has dined in various locations around the city and, each year on the Saturday before Christmas, processes to the bungalows pushing the city's mayor in a wheelbarrow to present seasonal fare to the residents.

The Smith Brothers

Artists have regularly been drawn towards to the district around Chichester, prospects of the city, views of the harbour and Downland scenes have been popular subjects. In the 18th century the city had its own family of painters in the Smith brothers. William, George and John Smith were the sons of William Smith of Chichester who was formerly a cooper, later a baker and minister of the Eastgate Baptist Chapel. His father, George Smith, had established the General Baptist church in Chichester during the 1670s and had been imprisoned for his beliefs.

The eldest of the Smiths was William (1707–64), who under the patronage of the Duke

of Richmond studied portrait painting in St Martin's, London. In 1730 he moved to Gloucester where he stayed for about eight years before returning to London. The city council own a copy of a portrait that William painted of the 2nd Duke in his garter robes. In addition to portraits he painted still life and landscapes. He later moved back to Chichester where he lived in a house belonging to the duke at Shopwyke, and where he died in 1764. His will shows that he had achieved considerable wealth and property during his career.

George Smith (1714–76), like his father, trained as a cooper. It was apparent that he shared his brother's talents as an artist and, in 1730, he abandoned his training and moved to study with his brother in Gloucester. He later became a landscape artist much admired by the Duke of Richmond. In the early 1740s he had a London studio, returning to Chichester in 1750 to live in North Street. In 1759 he was awarded a premium by the Society of Arts for one of his landscape paintings. George is said to have been

George, William and John Smith in a Contemporary mezzotint by William Pether.

an accomplished musician, who played the cello, and was a gifted poet. He did not marry until his 52nd year, his bride being Ruth Southen who was in her 30s. They had three daughters. The duke's patronage was continued by his son, the 3rd Duke, and on George's death in 1776, Lady Sarah Lennox, a sister of the duke, bought several of his pictures.

John Smith (1717–1764) the youngest of the brothers, also had their artistic talents. From about 1750 he shared George's North Street studio, and he also won the Society of Arts premium. John and William both died in 1764, George in 1776. They were buried in the Litten Cemetery in St Pancras. Although it has been removed from its original position their tombstone can still be seen alongside New Park Road.

Individually the Smiths may not have been artists of national stature, however, collectively their contribution to the nation's artistic heritage is more substantial. Their work influenced many others and has a significant place in the tradition of English landscape painting.

The Trial of the Smugglers

With its easy access across the channel to the ports in northern France, Sussex had been a centre for smugglers since the 13th century. In those times a bale a wool costing 1s 6d (7½p) carried a tax of £6 a bale when exported. Smuggling reached a new level in the middle of the 19th century. In addition to the export tax on wool, there were high taxes on the import of such commodities as wines and spirits, silks and lace. On tea, the tax was 4s 9d (24p) on a pound bag which could be purchased for 3d (2p) on the continent.

Various methods were employed to frustrate the smugglers, Sussex farmers living within 10 miles of the sea had to register their sheep at shearing time. In addition to the excisemen there were companies of troops stationed along the coast to prevent smuggling and ships patrolled

A booklet published at the time of the smuggler's trial proved to be a best seller, this illustration shows the breaking open of the Poole Custom House.

Customs Officer Galley and witness Chater are captured by the smugglers at The White Hart, Rowlands Castle.

the Channel. Penalties for smuggling were severe; those caught could expect the death penalty by hanging.

One case that occasioned national interest was the trial in Chichester in 1749 of members of the Hawkhurst gang. In November 1747 a gang of about 50 men broke into the Custom House at Poole and retrieved two tons of tea that had been captured earlier by custom men. One of the leaders, John Dymer, was arrested on suspicion and held in the gaol at Chichester. The case required a witness to testify against him, the authorities had such a man in Daniel Chater, a shoemaker from Fordingbridge, who had been given a small bag of the stolen tea by Dymer.

It was arranged for Chater to be brought to the Surveyor General of Customs, Major Battine who lived at East Marden, to give a statement. He was to be escorted by a customs officer, William Galley. On their journey they stayed at the White Hart Inn at Rowlands Castle, the landlady, widow Elizabeth Payne, had two sons who were both themselves smugglers. The word spread locally and soon a gang of smugglers assembled at the

inn. They plied Chater and Galley with drink and, tied together, they were taken by horseback towards Rake. Many unspeakable atrocities were committed on the unfortunate pair on the way. Galley died when his head hit the ground as he was slung under the horse. After drinking at the Red Lion the smugglers buried him in a foxhole in Harting Combe. Chater was kept tied up for three days in an outhouse and was then taken to Lady Holt Wood. After a savage beating he was thrown down a well where rocks were thrown on top of his body.

Although they lived in what we would consider fairly brutal times, the savageness of the crime shocked the people of the south, and much of the sympathy that the smugglers had enjoyed in the past turned into revulsion. Some who had been involved in smuggling turned king's evidence, resulting in the murderers being identified and rounded up. Their trial was set to be held in the Guildhall at Chichester on 18 January 1749.

The trial was held in a special assize, the judges Sir Thomas Birch, Sir Michael Foster and

Baron Clive were specially guarded as they made their way to the city via Hindhead and Midhurst. The Duke of Richmond entertained them at Goodwood before they convened the trial, the Dean preaching a sermon before the proceedings commenced. The defendants were Benjamin Tapner, a bricklayer from Aldingbourne, John Hammond, a labourer from South Bersted, John Cobby, William Jackson, a 50-year-old labourer from Aldsworth, William Carter, a thatcher from Rowlands Castle, Richard Mills, age 63, from Trotton and his son, also Richard Mills, aged 37 from Stedham, both described as colt breakers and horse dealers.

They were all found guilty and sentenced to be hanged and, except for the two Mills, their bodies were to be hung in chains. This was a punishment often reserved for highwaymen whereby their bodies were soaked in tar and hung up on a gibbet encased in an iron frame, usually at a place near to the scene of their crime, as a deterrent to others,

The execution was set for the day after the trial. William Jackson was found to have died in his cell when the blacksmith came on the evening before to measure him for the chains. The execution was held in a field on the Broyle by the Midhurst Road, about a mile outside the north gate of the city. A huge crowd of several thousand, possibly double the population of Chichester at the time, gathered to witness the hangings. Tradesmen sold fruit and pies, hawkers sold hastily printed broadsheets giving details of the prisoners and their crimes.

The gallows comprised two posts with a beam from which the nooses were hung, the men were stood on a cart which, after they were all give a

Chater is tortured at the Red Lion, Harting before being cruelly murdered.

This stone was erected on the site of the gallows, the inscription recorded their fate as a warning to others. The stone has been moved to the edge of the pavement in Broyle Road. Although the lettering has worn away over the years the painted board confirms the warning.

chance to make a last speech, was driven away leaving them to hang. The Rector of St Pancras, together with the Vicar of St Peter the Great, were present and are said to have given the Sacrament to some of the prisoners.

After the execution, Jackson's body was buried beneath the gallows and he thus escaped the irons that he had so feared. Carter's body was hung near his home at Rake, Cobby's and Hammond's at Selsey Bill, and Tapner's on the Trundle where, helped by an annual application of tar, it remained for 40 years until struck by lightning in 1749. An inscribed stone naming the men and detailing their crime was set up in Broyle Road, near to the site of the gallows, where it can still be seen. The nearby field, now part of the Barracks, was known for some time after as the Gallows Field.

The Workhouse

An earlier chapter mentioned the foundation by William Cawley in 1625 of an almshouse known as St Bartholomew's Hospital, sited in Broyle Road. When Cawley fled the country at the time of the Restoration it was conveyed to the mayor and corporation.

The mayor, Henry Peckham, reestablished the almshouse in 1681 as a workhouse for the poor. Bishop Henry King (1641–69) gave the sum of £100 towards its maintenance as did his successor Peter Gunning (1669–75). Few details of the house are known until 1753 when an Act of Parliament brought it under the control of a Board of guardians which included, among others, the mayor, the recorder, the justices of the peace and 30 persons that were elected from the eight parishes of the city.

The new body was empowered to raise funds for the upkeep of the workhouse by a taxation, or poor rate, upon the city's householders. It also had income from two fields near to the Dell Hole, although this ceased in 1782 when the Corporation sold the fields to raise money for the building of the new jail at Eastgate.

This 1904 postcard shows the cottage that is all that remains of the city's former pest house.

The minute books kept by the guardians tell us how one of the first actions of the new body was to commission two wings to be added to the building. Other works included the digging of wells, providing new ovens and the walling-in of the garden. In 1754 a brewhouse was built in the garden and, in 1764, it was decided to convert the kitchen into a court room for the use of the guardians and the Master. Another room was converted into a prison cell with iron bars fixed to the windows.

The administration of the workhouse was the responsibility of the Clerk to the guardians with day-to-day running carried out by the Master and Mistress. A medical officer was employed by the guardians, initially the post was held by an apothecary. Later a surgeon, Joseph Baker, was paid £20 per annum to carry out the duties; these included the care of the inmates of the Pest House in what is now College Lane. Although not part of the workhouse, this establishment was also administered by the guardians.

The daily life of the inmates was controlled by strict regulations. For instance in summer they were required to rise at 5am with prayers at 6am, then work until breakfast at 8am. This was followed by more work until evening prayers at 5pm, supper at 6pm and bed at 9pm. Children were to be washed and cleansed and their hair combed by 8am and then 'taught to read according to their several capacities'.

Those of the residents who broke the rules could expect harsh punishment, There is one instance where, for damaging the window shutter of her room, Lydia Smith, 'a poor pauper' was sentenced to be stripped to the waist and given 10 lashes of the cat of nine tails, administered by the town crier, who received 1s 6d for performing this duty. The workhouse guardians who passed this judgment also found it their obligation to be present to witness the punishment.

In the 1851 census 124 persons, described as paupers, were shown as being resident in the workhouse. The establishment survived into the early part of the 20th century by which time it catered mostly for tramps and vagrants. In the 1950s the building became the property of the Hospital Board who extended the premises to become the group laundry serving local hospitals.

A late 19th-century picture of East Street taken from the Cross.

A busy picture of North Street in 1963 taken by Geoffrey Claridge.

THE 19TH CENTURY

Chichester Society in 1800

During the early years of the 19th century, Chichester was in a state of transition from the mediaeval city into the township which survived well into the 20th century. The renovation and refronting of houses mentioned by Spershott 50 years earlier was still taking place. Although the contrast between the richer and poorer sections of society could not have been more marked, both seemed to have lived relatively closely together within Chichester. Many wealthy families lived within the city, particularly in the main streets and the Pallants. The less affluent lived in the suburbs and in the north-west sector around Tower Street and Chapel Street.

Following an upsurge in the population building beyond the city walls was becoming necessary. The building of housing outside the north gate, known as Somerstown, met the demand for rented accommodation. The roads in Somerstown of George Street, High Street and Cross Street formed a working-class community that was unique in Chichester and lasted virtually unchanged until after World War Two. In 1965 these streets and houses were demolished, a loss of which many still lament.

Now mostly used as professional offices, in 1800 these East Pallant houses were the homes of wealthy citizens.

Houses in George Street, Somerstown, await demolition in 1965 following the rehousing of the residents.

These shops in Broyle Road were part of the Somerstown suburb of the city.

The shops in the previous picture were demolished in 1965.

When Somerstown was cleared, the Methodist Church remained in use as a furniture depository until that too was pulled down to make way for new housing development.

These houses in Tower Street were built in the 19th century to house working-class families. Before that time the land was garden land belonging to the Dean and Chapter.

The wealthy citizens had a wide selection of activities available to allow them to enjoy a full and varied social life. Concerts were held regularly in the Assembly Rooms, the cost of admission being half a guinea (52p) to attend a season of six concerts. As many as 300 persons were often present to hear works performed by military bands, local musicians and by touring artistes. John Marsh, the composer and organist, who lived in North Pallant, arranged many of these events, often playing the organ which he had himself installed in the Assembly Rooms in 1791.

Dancing was a popular recreation, an advertisement for a 'Race Ball and Supper' which appeared in the *Sussex Chronicle* in April 1803. Held in the Assembly Rooms, gentlemen's tickets cost 15s (75p) and ladies 7s 6d (37p). Dancing went on until two o'clock in the morning and in Richard Dally's *Chichester Guide* of 1832 it is noted that 'The assemblies are attended by people of fashion and of the higher classes and tradesmen and their families are not admitted'.

In 1791 a purpose-built theatre was opened in South Street, it replaced the former malthouse that had been adapted for use as a theatre in 1764. Many of the most famous names in the theatrical world appeared on its stage, including Edmund Kean who played there in 1825. The theatre held up to 300 patrons, it closed in 1850 when the building was sold by auction, it is now used as a shopping arcade.

The more intellectual citizens were also catered for. In 1831 The Chichester Literary and Philosophical Society was founded, occupying a building in South Street. It included a museum and reading room for members and later merged with the Mechanics' Institute.

The poorer residents of the city also had their entertainments. James Spershott commented that

A contemporary print of the Chichester Theatre in South Street. The building has been used for various purposes since the days when such actors as Edmund Kean (1787–1833) appeared on its stage.

baiting' Records show that wrestling, cock-fighting and dog-fighting also took place within the city. Prize-fighting although illegal took place at venues kept secret until shortly before the event.

Churches and Chapels

Partly as a result of the population increase, churchgoers were so numerous throughout the 19th century that the existing churches and chapels proved insufficient to meet demand. To remedy this situation several new places of worship were built.

To meet the needs of Church of England worshippers St John's Chapel was built within the city in 1813. It was not attached to a parish, being a proprietary Anglican Chapel paid for by

the 'commonality were free in their conversation, calling one another by their first name and given to mean diversions such as bull-

When this picture was taken in the 1960s it was a furniture depository for Lewis & Co, whose showrooms were opposite.

The South Street Congregational Church, seen on the left, was built in 1892. In 1972 it joined with the Presbyterian church to become the United Reform Church. It survived until 1980 when it was pulled down to make way for shops. The members of the church amalgamated with those of the Methodist Church to build Christchurch in Market Avenue.

The Hornet Methodist Church closed for worship in 1956 and subsequently was sold for use as a Chinese takeaway.

public subscription. A new parish was formed when St Paul's Church was constructed in 1836 outside Northgate. This was also the case in 1869 when All Saints' Church at Portfield was built to cater for the growing population in the eastern suburbs. St George's Church was built in 1902 in Cleveland Road, to serve the Whyke area, which had been formed in 1893 when the ancient parish of Rumboldswyke was taken into the city's municipal boundaries.

The Non-Conformist community were served by Eastgate Chapel, Baffin's Hall and Providence Chapel, which have already been referred to. To these were added the Southgate Methodist Church, designed by Alexander Lander in 1876, the Congregational Church in South Street and new chapels in the Hornet and in Broyle Road.

St Peter the Great. This church, built in 1852, closed in 1978 and, after a period as a shopping mall, is now a public house.

It is a reflection that only one of these buildings, St Paul's Church, is still in use for the purpose for which it was built. The fates of others have been varied, the hornet chapel is a Chinese takeaway, Baffin's Hall is an auction room, Portfield Church is a museum, perhaps the most unlikely is that of St Peter the Great in West Street, which became the Slurping Toad public house.

The Care of the Sick

The incidence of typhoid and cholera within the city during the latter years of the 18th century was a cause of much concern. The number of cases of smallpox, which had previously caused many deaths, had been reduced as a result of inoculation from 168 deaths in 1722 to just 24 in 1775. By the middle 1800s Chichester had one of the highest rates of cholera in the country, due mainly to the fact that there were no main drains or water supply. Water was drawn from wells in the same ground that cesspits were discharging into.

A public dispensary had been established in 1784 in some cottages in Broyle Road, on the site now known as Infirmary Terrace, by Chichester practitioner Dr Thomas Sanden and William Walker, the rector of the parishes of St Pancras and St Mary's, Rumboldswyke. It served the needs of the sick poor. Records show that of 160 patients admitted in the first year, 91 were cured, 65 'relieved' and four died.

The early 19th-century boom in the population of Chichester made it soon apparent that there was need for a much larger establishment. A public appeal was made, a sum of £8,500 was subscribed, including £600 donated by the Duke of Richmond. The new hospital was designed by a local architect, George Draper, who had been responsible for several churches in

An 1848 lithograph of Sir John Forbes by T.H. Maguire. (*The Wellcome Institute*)

the area. It cost £7,454 to build and was open for its first patients by 31 October 1826.

The main promoter of the scheme to build the hospital was Sir John Forbes (1787–1861).

Forbes first came to Chichester as a general practitioner in 1822, he had qualified as a physician at Edinburgh University having previously served as a naval surgeon. The new premises were built on the same site as the former dispensary, the foundation stone being laid by the Duke of Richmond on 10 June 1825. The establishment was known as the Chichester Infirmary and Forbes was appointed as the first consulting physician. He became celebrated as a pioneer in the use of the stethoscope as an aid to diagnosis, it being said that he first experimented with the instrument in Chichester. He left the city in 1840 to pursue a distinguished career in medicine and was knighted in 1853.

The hospital found its own solution to the problem of the suspect water supply by brewing beer on the premises, every male patient had one pint a day and females a half-pint. The old brew house can still be seen on the site.

The Infirmary became a respected voluntary hospital serving the local community. The original building was enlarged several times in the 19th century and in 1913 was extended and completely modernised. The building was reopened on 2 August that year by George V

George V reopened the West Sussex Hospital in August 1913 and gave it its 'Royal' title.

who conferred the title 'Royal' to the hospital's name as a memorial to his father Edward VII, thus it became the Royal West Sussex Hospital.

The first matron, Mrs Rogers, was given a wisteria plant, imported from China, and one of the first seen in this country. It was planted against the front wall of the new building and is reputed to be the oldest-known specimen in England. When the new extension was built to St Richard's Hospital in 1997 a cutting was planted there.

The Royal West was originally a voluntary hospital, local practitioners, who were often themselves on the staff, referred patients who paid what they could afford. Later there was a Hospital Savings Association whose members paid weekly towards their care should they later become patients.

For many years this was the city's only hospital; besides treating the citizens it was a training hospital for nurses. At the beginning of the World War Two, hutted wards were built in the grounds in anticipation of wounded troops being brought back from the battle fronts.

The hospital closed in 1985 and the building has been converted into luxury apartments and flats, it is known as Forbes Place commemorating the name of Sir John, its founder.

The Dukes of Richmond in the 19th Century

The 4th Duke of Richmond succeeded to the title, aged 42, in 1806 on the death of his uncle. In 1790 he had been chosen as the MP for Chichester, holding the seat until his elevation to the dukedom. In 1818 he was appointed Governor-General of the British settlements in North America. It was whilst in Canada, in 1819, that he was bitten by a tame fox and infected

A print of Goodwood racecourse in 1853.

with rabies. He returned to the town of Richmond, that had been named after him, but survived only a few days before dying of hydrophobia.

As a young man the 5th Duke chose to follow a military career. Despite being severely wounded in 1819, at the Battle of Orthez in the Peninsular War, he was able to remain in the Army, ultimately retiring with the rank of lieutenant-colonel. As the Earl of March he had been elected, at the age of 21, to represent Chichester in Parliament. On becoming duke he took his place in the House of Lords, serving as Postmaster-General. On the death of his mother in 1842 he inherited the Gordon Estates which enabled him to complete additions to Goodwood House.

Despite his injuries preventing him from riding he owned several racehorses and was a successful breeder. It was the 5th Duke who first introduced horse-racing to Goodwood. He was a member, and one time president of the MCC and is credited with forming Sussex County Cricket Club. He died in 1860 and is buried in Chichester Cathedral. His marriage in 1817 to Lady Caroline Paget had produced 11 children.

His son was 42 when he succeeded as the 6th Duke. Almost immediately he was involved in fundraising for the rebuilding of the Cathedral spire, he chaired the committee supervising the work and laid the foundation stone of the new structure. Whilst Earl of March he had served for 20 years as the MP for the County. He continued his political career in the House of Lords, serving as the President of the Board of Trade and in 1870 was appointed leader of the Conservative Party. During his ownership of the Goodwood Estate over 400 houses, known locally as Duke's Cottages, were built as homes for the estate workers. He was 85 when he died in 1903, like his ancestors he was buried in the family tomb in the Cathedral. A stained glass window was installed in his memory.

Law and Order

Crime was dealt with severely in the early part of the 19th century, wrongdoers could expect to receive publicly-administered corporal punishment. Drunkenness was a major problem throughout the century. With 60 public houses and over 30 ale houses within the city there was no shortage of places to find refreshment. The situation was exacerbated every other Wednesday when the Market took place, farmers and traders from the outlying villages would join the local drinkers.

Vandalism might be considered by some to be a modern-day malaise. However in 1802 a reward of five guineas was offered for information leading to the conviction of persons found breaking or stealing lamps. The presence of soldiers from the barracks added to the city's

The city stocks, last used in 1852 to punish 'Shadow' Mason for drunkenness, are now on display in the District Museum. (*CDM*)

An 1895 picture of North Street in which the Wheatsheaf Hotel can be clearly seen.

S. CROSBIE

HOSIER

A 1910 view of the police station at Eastgate. The building was built as the city gaol in 1783. (*Keith Smith*)

sold in 1806 as being 'useless for the purpose intended'

In 1828 the council ordered the construction of a set of wheeled stocks for the punishment of wrong-doers. These were last used in April 1852 when Henry 'Shadow' Mason was sentenced to spend two hours in them by the Cross for drunkenness.

In 1836, following an Act of Parliament, the council's Watch Committee formed the Chichester city police force. It comprised one superintendent, a sergeant and seven constables. The constables' pay was 14 shillings (70p) a week from Michaelmas to Lady Day and 10 shillings and sixpence (52p) for the rest of the year. By 1850 the strength of the force was down to just three. The superintendent, Richard Greene, also ran a business as a hatter in North Street; he was assisted by Sergeant Stringer and a constable who lived in a house in Chapel Street in which had a room for use as a lock-up. None of the police at this time wore uniforms.

problems. On St David's Day in 1807, the Monmouth and Brecon Militia's celebrations in the Wheatsheaf Inn in North Street resulted in one constable, Mr Frogbrook, receiving a bayonet wound and another having three ribs broken.

The city council found it necessary in 1819 to appoint a beadle or street-keeper to clear the city of beggars. He was duly sworn in by the magistrates as a special constable and paid two shilling a week. This post was in addition to the two watchmen who patrolled the main streets during the nights. A watch house was built in 1821 'for the purpose of confining disturbers of the peace within the city at night time' It apparently replaced the iron cage that was provided in the Council House and which was

When the West Sussex police force was formed in 1857, the Chichester authorities decided that their force should be updated. Uniforms were issued consisting of a top hat, a frock coat with the officers number displayed on the high collar and a black leather belt with the force's coat of arms on the buckle. The number of constables was brought back to seven. The Superintendent, Mr Everitt, lived on the premises at the Eastgate prison, where the city force had their headquarters. Sergeant Stringer was the sole survivor of the early establishment.

In George Tippen's memoirs of his boyhood in the 1870s, he recounts how the constables carried long poles, mainly he said, to keep the

These eight men were members of the city police force in 1889. Their colleague PC North was presumably on duty, Second from the right, front row is Superintendent Arthur Pratt. Note the station cat being held by PC Goff. (*CDM*)

naughty boys of the city in order and deter them from loitering on street corners. There is a record that on Sloe Fair night in 1880, Police Constable Phillips, PC4, was found to be drunk on duty, this not being the first time that PC Phillips had been found the worse for drink on duty. In his letter of apology to the Watch Committee he made a promise of future good conduct, his punishment is not recorded. However when, in 1889, the city police force was disbanded, becoming absorbed into the county force, Phillips was one of the officers transferred.

Transport
Travel between towns in the early 19th century was by stagecoach. The roads were kept in order by the Turnpike Trusts and paid for by tolls. The road between Chichester and Bosham had three tollgates, the first at Westgate, the next at Fishbourne and one at Broadbridge. The gates were let out annually by the trustees, the successful bidders keeping the takings from their gate. In 1837 the Westgate tollgate was let for £900, Fishbourne for £600 and Broadbridge for £200.

To get to London there were two stage coaches leaving the city each day, one from the Dolphin Hotel in West Street and one from the Swan in East Street. One ran through Petworth, the other through Midhurst. In each case another coach made a return journey the same day. Coaches left Chichester at about nine in the morning, arriving in the capital at about five in the evening, a journey of eight hours, which included a break to take lunch and change the horses.

The stage coach no longer departed from the Dolphin by the time that this picture was taken in Goodwood week, 1912. Clearly the proprietors now catered for the latest form of transport, the motor car.

Whereas large cargoes and heavy goods had previously been carried by sea, the opening of the Canal in 1821 provided an alternative mode for a short while. From 1846 the railway gave a faster, less expensive means for the conveyance of goods. Travellers found that travel by train was quicker, more comfortable and cost less than the stage coaches. We will see how, 100 years later when competition from the bus companies had caused the closure of the branch railway lines, transport returned to the roads.

Chichester Canal

Since Roman times the Port of Chichester was one of the busiest in the country. Cargoes of grain, timber and wool were among the goods exported, and imports included coal, wines, cloth and building materials. Although there were some storage sheds at Dellquay, Apuldram and Itchenor most goods were transported to and from Chichester by land.

The idea of building a canal to join the city to the harbour was first suggested in the 16th century. In 1585 the mayor and corporation obtained an Act of Parliament which would have allowed them to cut a channel from Dellquay to the city walls. The cost of the work at that time prevented the scheme proceeding. In the preamble to the Act, mention was made to the bad state of the road between the city and the port, and the lack of accommodation for both men and goods at Dellquay.

Towards the end of the 18th century canal building was taking place throughout the country. Carriage by canal was slow, but the size of the loads that could be transported made them competitive when compared to roads. In 1817 a scheme to construct a canal from the harbour at Birdham to the River Arun at Ford was approved by Parliament. It was part of a project that would allow goods to be carried from Portsmouth Harbour to London via the Rivers Arun and Wey.

A sailing barge makes its way towards the canal basin in the 1990s, possibly with a load of gravel.

Among the advantages put forward by the promoters were the easy transportation of agricultural produce from West Sussex to serve the Navy at Portsmouth, and also the provision of a safe route between Portsmouth and London. This would avoid the perils of taking the stormy channel route, and the danger of attack from French warships. It was also suggested that the cultivation of the adjoining countryside would be improved as a result of the more efficient conveyance of manure. As most towns did not, at that time, have sewers, the type of 'manure' referred to can only be speculated upon.

The Portsmouth and Arundel Navigation Company had among its directors George Wyndham, Earl of Egremont, and W. Poyntz, the MP for Chichester, as well as two local landholders over whose property the canal was to pass, General Crosbie of Donnington and William Cutfield of Climping.

An important feature of the proposal, as far as the merchants of Chichester were concerned, was

The Canal, looking overgrown with weed in 1904. In the background can be seen the chimney and a gasometer of the Chichester Gas Works.

the cutting of a spur from the canal at Hunston to a basin to be created near to the city at Southgate.

Work was started in September 1818 and was complete by December 1821 when water was let into the basin. The Chichester branch was 15 metres (50ft) wide and 2.4 metres (8ft) deep. There were six swing bridges constructed over the canal, named after six of the scheme's leading supporters, Egremont, Casher, Dudley, Cutfield, Crosbie and Poyntz. The last three names were reused in 1968 for street names when new houses were built at Donnington, near to the canal.

Before the canal opened colliers could sail no further up the harbour than Itchenor, their cargoes were then transferred to lighters and taken to Dellquay. After being unloaded the onward transport by road included having turnpike tolls to pay. The new canal enabled vessels of up to 100 tons to deliver direct to the city. Joseph Pennicott, a Chichester coal merchant, acquired two sailing barges both capable of going to sea.

Among other goods carried by the barges between the harbour and Chichester were timber, lime, bricks, sand and gravel. In 1823 Chichester Gas Works were opened adjoining the basin and a Mr Cover established his timber wharf nearby.

The canal enterprise never became the commercial success that the investors expected, and the company never paid a dividend. In 1846 the London, Brighton and South Coast Railway reached Chichester. The effect upon the canal was almost immediate. By 1855 the Ford to Hunston section was abandoned and in 1888 the company was wound up. The Chichester branch was still used for some years, since it was still the most effective way to bring coal to the gas works. In 1906 the Combe Brothers, of Bosham, brought a load of shingle from the harbour in their sailing barge, which was the last recorded cargo unloaded at the basin.

In recent years interest has grown in the use of the canal for recreational purposes, and it is a popular venue for anglers. The Chichester Canal Society has been formed to preserve and exploit its leisure potential. They have had it dredged and cleared it of weeds that threatened to choke it. During summer months trips can be made from the basin to Hunston in a pleasure boat.

The Railway

Throughout the years 1830–50, railway building proceeded throughout the country at a tremendous rate. By 1835, despite opposition from the owners of canals, turnpike trusts and coaching interests, 54 railways had been approved by Parliament. In the years 1836 and 1837 a further 54 Railway Acts were passed and by 1848 over 5,000 miles of railways were operating in the United Kingdom.

In Sussex the first railway line, which ran from Hove to Shoreham, was opened in 1840, followed, in 1841, by the London to Brighton line. Construction progressed along the south coast reaching Chichester on 8 June 1846 when the London, Brighton and South Coast Railway Company opened the 28-mile long stretch of line from Brighton. By March the following year the line was extended to Havant and in June the stretch to Portsmouth was completed.

A branch line was built later in the 19th century connecting Chichester to Midhurst and, in 1897, a light railway connected the city to Selsey. The first of these was the Midhurst Line which opened in July 1881. Midhurst already had two railway stations, one serving a branch line from Pulborough via Fittleworth and Petworth, the other a track to Petersfield. Permission for the line was obtained by the LBSCR in 1876, the intention was to run through trains from Chichester to Pulborough and thence to Horsham.

The new line branched off the main south coast line at Fishbourne. The Fishbourne

The old railway station was built in 1846 in an Italianate style. Had it been renovated it could have added to the city's architectural heritage. Sadly it was demolished in 1961 to make way for the new station. (*Charles Attwell Collection*)

A 1910 picture of the station, note the gas lighting and the milk churns awaiting collection. (*Charles Attwell Collection*)

This fine three-storey station was built for the village of Lavant.

Crossing signal box controlled the points giving access to the track. The line was a major engineering construction. Three tunnels had to be built, at West Dean, Singleton and Cocking, to enable it to cross the South Downs. Stations were built at Lavant, Singleton and Cocking and a new station was built at Midhurst 500 yards to the east of the original.

Singleton Station was a large building with two platforms, each with elaborate canopies. Over threequarters of a mile of sidings were capable of holding up to 14 trains on the days when Goodwood races were taking place. Today the station has been converted to a winery serving a vineyard established nearby. It is difficult to believe that thousands of racegoers would arrive at the station to take cabs or walk up to the racecourse. Members of the British and other royal families alighted on the platforms. Edward VII was a regular visitor to West Dean House and a special royal train bearing his coat of arms on the engine would bring him to Singleton.

By the 1930s the line had fallen into decline, being unable to compete with the more regular bus services. Even on Goodwood race days it became easier for patrons to take the train to Chichester and get to the racecourse by bus or cab. The line closed to passenger traffic in 1935, although it continued to be used for freight. During World War Two the tunnels were used by ammunition trains. After the war the line was opened once again for goods traffic. On 19 November 1951, after a torrential storm the previous night, an embankment at Cocking was washed away. Although the driver and crew were able to leap clear the engine plunged into the crater that had appeared. The line was never fully reopened, although trains used the line seasonally, between Chichester and Lavant, for the transport of sugar beet until 1972. Part of the remaining track was later diverted to serve pits at Lavant, the 'gravel trains' running daily

The Selsey Tram passes over the canal lift bridge at Hunston drawn by *Sidlesham*, soon after the locomotive's introduction to the tramway in 1907. (*David Bathurst*)

The crew of the Selsey tram, guard King, ticket collector Barnes, driver Johnson and fireman Gilbert pose alongside the locomotive *Selsey* in this photograph taken at the Chichester terminus in about 1900. (*David Bathurst*)

The Chichester terminus of the Selsey Tramway at Southgate. The two gas works gasometers are clearly visible. This branch line was the base for an artillery train in World War Two.

between the pits and the washing plant at Drayton. This trade ceased in the 1990s after which the lines were removed. The route of the line has recently been converted into a pedestrian and cycling track known as Centurion Way.

The railway from Chichester to Selsey had been approved in an Act of Parliament of 1888. It did not proceed at that time as the cost proved prohibitive and it was not until the Light Railways Bill of 1895 that it became a viable proposition. The Hundred of Manhood and Selsey Tramway Company was formed in 1896 and, by 27 August 1897, the official opening of the line took place, with the first train travelling from Chichester to Selsey.

The Selsey Tramway station at Chichester was little more than a shed sited to the south of the main line station. On leaving the station the tram took a sharp turn left, crossing the main road at Stockbridge, where a loud whistle from the engine would warn road users of its approach. In the case of goods trains, which had to build up speed to tackle the incline, the station master would cycle down to the crossing to halt road

vehicles. In 1932, following several incidents and near misses, new regulations were introduced requiring that the train should stop and the engine's fireman should alight with a red flag or lamp to halt the traffic.

The tram crossed the Chichester Canal at Hunston where a drawbridge was constructed to allow the passage of the barges which still brought cargoes from the harbour at Birdham to the city. In the early years the train was drawn by steam locomotives. The journey time for the seven miles between Chichester and Selsey was about 30 minutes, although the record was said to have been set at 17 minutes, travelling at a speed of about 24mph. In 1928 rail cars were introduced. These had the appearance of single-deck buses adapted to run on rails, and were driven by petrol engines.

The enterprise ran into financial difficulties in the early 1930s as passenger numbers dropped in the face of competition from bus companies. Buildings and rolling stock were in need of repair and replacement. After being under control of a receiver for two years the Selsey

Tram ceased to run on 19 January 1935, after 38 years. Today a reminder of the former line is the Selsey Tram public house, which is sited near to the point where the track crossed the main road at Stockbridge.

Huskisson

In the north aisle of Chichester Cathedral there stands the imposing marble statue of William Huskisson. Dressed in a toga, in the style of a Roman senator, one can have no doubt that this was a man of some importance. The plaque on the base records that Huskisson represented the city of Chichester in Parliament, and that he met his death in a railway accident.

In fact William Huskisson achieved the questionable distinction of being the first person to die in this way. The incident occurred on 15 September 1830, the occasion was the official opening of the Liverpool and Manchester Railway. Among those present were the Prime Minister (the Duke of Wellington), Secretary of State, Sir Robert Peel, local civic dignitaries, religious leaders, ambassadors and the engineers responsible for the project, George and Robert Stephenson. Huskisson, who was the president of the Board of Trade and had been a Cabinet minister since 1823, was invited together with his wife Elizabeth.

Eight trains were assembled at Edge Hill Station in Liverpool to make the 30-mile journey. The Duke of Wellington's carriage was in the train pulled by George Stephenson's locomotive, *The Northumbrian.* So that the duke and his party could be seen by the occupants of the other trains his train was running on the northerly line whilst the others followed on the parallel southern line. The route was packed by cheering crowds and, for an hour, all went to plan with the locomotive halting at Parkside Station, about halfway along the route, to take in water.

Whilst the train was halted, several passengers, including Huskisson, disobeyed

In his Cathedral memorial, Huskisson is depicted dressed in a toga in the style of a Roman senator to denote his standing as an eminent statesman.

instructions and alighted from their carriages to stretch their legs. As they stood conversing between the two lines a shout went up 'Get in! Get in!' as another of the trains, pulled by *The Rocket* was approaching on the other line. While others scrambled to safety Huskisson, who is known to have had a 'gammy' leg, slipped and fell into the path of the oncoming locomotive. He was seriously injured, with his leg smashed and badly bleeding, and was attended by Lord Wilton, a surgeon, who applied a tourniquet to the severed artery.

Huskisson was placed into a carriage pulled by *The Northumbrian.* It sped at the hitherto unheard-of speed of 36mph, to Eccles where Huskisson was carried into a vicarage where doctors, who had been summoned from Manchester, examined him. There was little that they could do. After receiving the Holy Sacrament from the vicar and dictating a codicil to his will, he died that evening.

Those that remained upon the scene made the decision to carry on with the planned event. Today a memorial tablet is to be seen by the place where Huskisson met his fate. The Cathedral statue, by J.E. Carew, a leading sculptor of the age, was erected as a tribute from the city to one who had served as their MP for 10 years.

The Fall of the Spire

On Thursday 21 February 1861 at about 1.30pm the spire of the Cathedral fell, taking with it the central tower and most of the roof of the north transept. The effect it had on the city's residents was as one of bereavement. Many were in tears, the Bishop, Ashurst Turner Gilbert, went into the streets giving comfort to the apparently grief-stricken citizens.

Initially the blame was put on those responsible for removing the Arundel Screen the previous year. This masonry structure had stood between the western piers of the central tower and, in fact, it was not attached to them but its removal had exposed the state of the piers and, rather than causing it, had alerted the Cathedral authorities to the impending danger.

This photograph gives an indication of the damage to the inside of the Cathedral. It was taken several weeks after the incident when the rubble had been cleared.

A contemporary print from the *Illustrated London News* published a week after the fall of the spire.

The faults that caused the fall dated to the first construction of the building and had been compounded over the centuries. The original Norman tower had been seated on unsuitable foundations and the cores of the supporting piers were composed of rubble set in poor quality mortar and offered little strength to the structure. Following the fire of 1187 the piers were recased in an outer skin of masonry which was not bonded to the core. The tower was

A contemporary picture showing the new spire encased in scaffolding on the day when the weather vane was re-fixed to the pinnacle.

heightened considerably 200 years later and, in the 14th century, the spire was added. In the 18th century parts of the piers were cut away to make provision for the choir stalls and to give access to the organ loft.

When the Arundel Screen was taken away in 1860, the fissures that were exposed caused great consternation. Dozens of workmen were called in, including sailors from Portsmouth. Massive timbers were erected to support the tower arches whilst the piers were repaired, and struts were positioned externally to prop up the structure. It was all to no avail as the walls of the tower began to bulge. On the night of 20 February, fierce gales caused the tower and spire to rock visibly and large pieces of stone fell. The same night in London a storm destroyed the north wing of the Crystal Palace.

The following morning the workmen, who had been on the site until 3am, returned at 6.30. Additional struts were erected to support the tower. At noon the men went to their lunch, but Mr Bushby, the builder in charge of the operation refused to let them into the building on their return. The news spread rapidly and crowds gathered, waiting for the inevitable. At 1.30 the spire leant slightly to the south-west then descended, telescoping into the tower. Some spectators described it as being like a large ship sinking at sea.

Five days after the spire fell, a public meeting was held in the council chamber with the mayor, Robert Raper, in the chair. It was decided that an appeal be launched to rebuild it. A committee was appointed with the Duke of Richmond as chairman. Gilbert Scott was appointed as the architect for the project. On 6 March, Albert, the Prince Consort, visited the ruins. He donated £100 towards the restoration fund and Queen Victoria gave £250. By the end of June over £28,000 had been given towards the estimated cost of £50,000.

The contract was given to Messrs J. & W. Beanland of Bradford and work began in August. The first task after clearing the rubble was to construct new foundations. By 2 May 1865 the tower had risen to above the roof of the the main body of the Cathedral, and the foundation stone of the new spire was laid by the duke.

On 28 June 1866 crowds gathered to see the 'crowning' of the spire with the weather cock, which had been recovered from the ruins, repaired and regilded. It was a day of great rejoicing with processions, bands, an open-air concert and fireworks in the park. The inmates of the workhouse were given a dinner of roast beef and plum pudding.

There was still much interior work to be done,

Another print from the *Illustrated London News* showing the restoration of the weathercock to the spire on 28 June 1866.

and it was not until November 1867 that a service of thanksgiving could be held to mark the final restoration of the building. Over 200 clergy, including nine bishops, were joined by civic leaders, and more than 2,500 people who crowded into the building. It had taken just three months under six years for the restoration to be completed and the final cost of the work was £70,000.

Bishop Otter College

William Otter was the Bishop of Chichester from 1836 to 1840. Before his appointment he had been a schoolmaster and the principal of King's College, London. During his time at Chichester he was active in the campaign for provision of education for all. It is told that among those attending the bishop's funeral were several who shared his ideals. After the service they took the opportunity to hold a meeting in the Cathedral library. As a result, a committee was formed with the aim of establishing a teacher-training school as a memorial to William Otter.

In April 1840 the new college opened in premises over Edney's Stores in St Martin's Lane; the site is now part of Marks and Spencer's shop. Initially three students enrolled for training, but by 1848 some 40 had qualified to be teachers. In

A bust of Bishop William Otter in the Cathedral. The bishop's abiding interest in education was recognised by the institution of the teachers' training college named after him.

justify its continuation and the reluctant decision was made to close it.

In 1873 the college was reopened as a training college for women, preference being given to the daughters of clergy. Admission was by examination and the successful students, who had to be at least 18 years old, were charged £20 per annum for the two-year course. The college began with 26 students – by 1876, when the premises were enlarged, there were 40. Besides the basic curriculum, which included English, mathematics and religious knowledge, other subjects taught were geometry, botany and needlecraft. Two hours each day were allocated to physical recreation, such as tennis, country walks and dancing. Among the facilities provided in the 1876 enlargement was a school for children from the city in which the pupil teachers could gain practical experience in the classroom.

Under the leadership of the principal, Revd Edwin Hammonds, from 1897 to 1919 the student roll increased from 40 to over 150. In 1901 the college was enlarged to meet this growth and four new dormitories were added, together with an assembly hall and a science laboratory. The college formed links with local junior schools whereby students could obtain direct classroom experience.

1850 the college moved to newly-built premises in what is now know as College Lane.

Known as the Bishop Otter Memorial Training College for Schoolmasters, the institution accepted only male teachers. By 1867 there were insufficient students enrolling to the college to

A 1861 print of the college soon after its building.

A 1913 postcard view of the college showing the chapel in the background.

During the years leading up to World War Two the establishment was enlarged several times as student numbers and needs increased. In 1942 the college was taken over by the Royal Air Force and initially used as accommodation for some 500 members of the Women's Auxillary Air Force. In 1944 the Tangmere air station's operations room was transferred from St James' School to the college's assembly hall. During the Allied invasion of Normandy in June 1944, over 50 squadrons of aircraft were controlled from this room. During this time the college was transferred to Stockwell College in South London, which had itself been evacuated.

The college returned to its own premises in 1945 and in 1948 Miss K.M.E. Murray became the principal. By the time she retired in 1970, by then Dr Murray, the college was co-educational – male students were first admitted in 1960 – and the courses included the four-year B.Ed qualification. The student population had risen to over 600.

In 1976, Bishop Otter College merged with the Bognor Regis College to form the West Sussex Institute of Higher Education. In 1999 the college was granted power to award degrees and the

The college principal, the Revd Edwin Hammond, with his staff in 1908.

Teachers in training, the students of the Long Dormitory in 1911.

Privy Council approved the change of name to University College Chichester. Over 4,000 students are currently on full and part-time degree courses; seven per cent of these are overseas students.

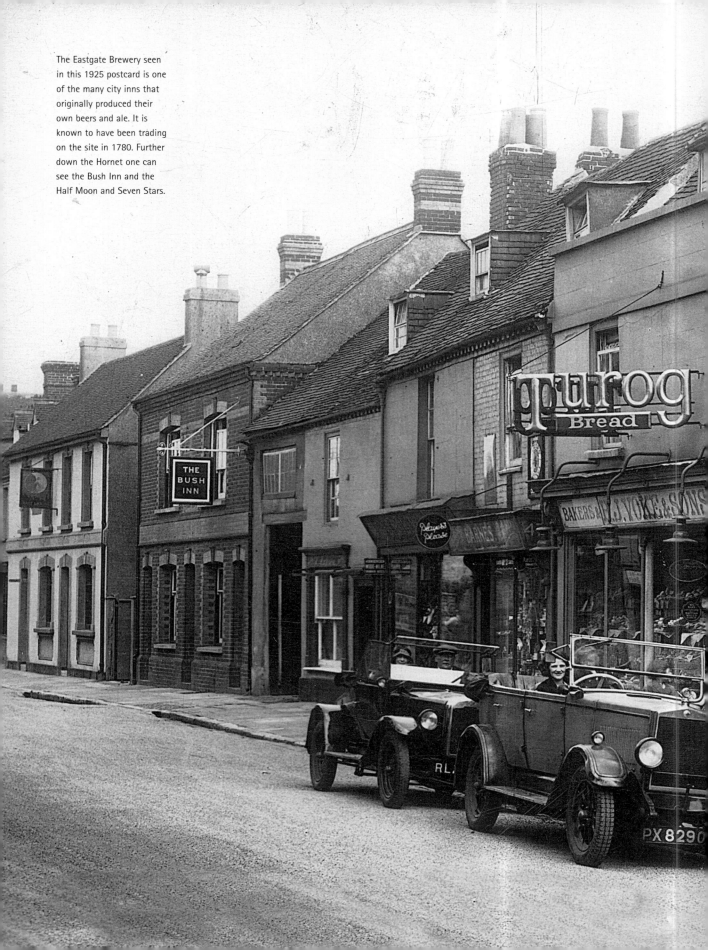

The Eastgate Brewery seen in this 1925 postcard is one of the many city inns that originally produced their own beers and ale. It is known to have been trading on the site in 1780. Further down the Hornet one can see the Bush Inn and the Half Moon and Seven Stars.

Chichester's Drink Problem

William Hudson was a popular writer in the late 19th century. He was a learned naturalist who wrote about his travels throughout England, and the book, *Nature in Downland*, published in 1900, described his journey through Sussex. However, his impressions of Chichester were far from complimentary, his particular concern being the amount of liquor sold and consumed within the city.

Hudson reported that he was conscious of an odour pervading all about the city. He described it as 'an effluvium ascending in warm and damp weather from long-covered old forgotten cesspools'. This aroma, he claimed, together with the sights that met the eye, induced within visitors a depression known to sufferers as 'the chichesters'.

The sights that he referred to were the many public houses that were to be found in the city, and the number of men that loitered about the streets obviously under the influence of alcoholic excess. In a town with a male population of about 3,000 there were over 70 public houses and many wine and spirit merchants. Hudson reported that to keep these houses in business an immense quantity of liquor was consumed.

From eight in the morning until 11 at night the bars were open with men standing 'pipe in mouth and tankard in hand'. In the streets and around the Market Cross one could see groups of 'the most utterly drink degraded wretches it is possible to find anywhere in the kingdom, men with soulless bloated faces and watery eyes, dressed like tramps'.

Suffering from an attack of 'the chichesters', Hudson fled into the Cathedral. Unfortunately he had chosen market day and his visit was unceremoniously ended when his guide was called away to rid the precincts of a drove of pigs that had broken in. There is no record of William Hudson ever making a return visit to the city.

The picture that Hudson painted was one that is unrecognisable to us today. However, when one considers that the city did not have a drainage system, with sewage accumulating in cesspits and soaking into the subsoil, perhaps the residents were wise in choosing not to drink water from wells, finding beer a purer and more acceptable beverage.

Markets

It will be apparent from earlier chapters that much of Chichester's prosperity through the ages has been due to its position as a market town. As early as the 12th century, markets had been held in the main streets. The old council house which stood in the middle of North Street was a two storey timber building with the council chamber on the first floor. The open sided lower floor was used as a corn market. The structure is shown on Norden's 1595 map of the city and Spershott noted its demolition in 1731 when the present Council House was opened.

The Market Cross was provided by Bishop Storey in 1501 so that traders could have a place under cover to sell their goods. Often the wives of farmers would sell their produce, while their husbands sold their animals in the streets. This facility was lost in 1808, when the Butter Market, built in North Street by the City Council at a cost of £1,522, to a design by John Nash was opened. The Butter Market catered for traders selling fish, poultry, butter, vegetables and other locally-sourced commodities.

The prosperous corn traders of the city had subscribed towards the building of the Corn Exchange in 1833. Today the building houses McDonald's restaurant. In its day it was a busy centre where farmers and merchants carried on their business.

Despite these facilities, in the 19th century the city's beast markets where still being held each Wednesday in the main streets. North Street was the site of the pig market and in East Street, from

The Market House, known locally as the Buttermarket, was built to a design by John Nash in 1808. The upper storey was added in 1900 to provide a technical institute and art school.

Aldermen and councillors assemble with the mayor as he formally cuts the first sod to mark the start of the construction of the new market.

A picture taken before 1872 showing the cattle market being held in North Street. The Anchor public house on the right is now Turner's shoe shop. (*CDM*)

Farmers gather round the auctioneer at a sale of cattle in 1902. (*CDM*)

Auctioneer Walter Stride taking bids at the sheep sales in the market, in the early 1930s. (*CDM*)

Market day in Eastgate
Square taken about the
same time as the picture on
page 112. The railings that
prevented the cattle from
straying on to the pavement
can be seen. (*CDM*)

The Fat Stock Society held its annual show at the market in December 1962, these sheep won first prize in their class.

Little London to the Cross, wattle hurdles were erected overnight to form pens for sheep. Cattle were sold further down in East Street between Little London and Eastgate Square. Sometimes the trading spread further afield, to the disgust of the bishop who, in 1859, complained that the sheep market had begun to extend into West Street.

In 1859 the town clerk drew the Corporation's attention to the disgusting state of the streets following the weekly market. The residents of St John's Street had posts and chains put up at the junction with East Street to prevent the animals from entering. An article published in 1865 in the *Daily Telegraph* commented with surprise that Chichester should still 'suffer a cattle market to be held within its walls'

Finally in 1867, following the death of a man, gored by a bull, and injuries to others from oxen running wild, a petition from residents was made to the Corporation requesting that the markets be held elsewhere. Although many shopkeepers objected, fearing loss of business, it was decided that the market should be removed from the main streets to fields outside the east gate.

A Bill was passed by Parliament to permit the new market. On 7 May 1870 the mayor, Alderman Samuel Merricks, together with the full council, carried out the solemn ceremony of cutting the first sod of grass. A silver spade was used and champagne broken over the wheelbarrow containing the piece of turf. The market was completed and opened for business on Wednesday 10 May 1871, this was an occasion for further municipal ceremony and celebration. A licence was given to a Mr Kennet to sell ale from a booth to 'frequenters of the Market'.

The market survived, almost unchanged, until the latter half of the 20th century. Livestock was

A fine picture taken by Chichester photographer Huskinson of the 1897 commemorative north gate erected for the diamond jubilee of Queen Victoria.

This 1911 reconstruction of the east gate was considered to be an accurate replica of the original.

sold, by auction each Wednesday and on alternate weeks there was a section for the sale of domestic animals and 'dead-stock'. This last category covered almost any item and many local children obtained their first bicycles at these events.

In the 1980s Chichester District Council, as owners of the site, wished to redevelop the land and put forward a proposal comprising a new supermarket and housing.

After much public debate, and opposition from, among others, the Chichester Society, the scheme was abandoned. However the market was closed in 1990 and replaced with a car park. A traders' market is held on the historic location twice a week.

The Commemorative Gates

In June 1887 the whole country joined in celebrating Queen Victoria's Golden Jubilee, the 50th anniversary of her accession to the throne. In Chichester, among other celebrations, decorated archways were erected on the sites of the city's former gates. This started a tradition that was repeated for the Diamond Jubilee in 1897 and for the coronations of Edward VII in 1902 and George V in 1911. Using such materials as timber and canvas, local businessmen took control of the design and construction of the 'gates', each competing to provide the most lavish structure.

The city's photographers soon realised the potential business to be gained from the crowds

The reconstruction of the south gate for the coronation of George V in 1911, the building on the right is St Richard's Roman Catholic Church, demolished in 1958.

Also for George V's coronation this photograph, like the previous one, was taken by Russell's, a well-known Chichester firm. It shows the north gate.

In the same series as the previous pictures this shows the west gate, and is a fine example of the photographer's skill.

The scene at Eastgate for the coronation of George VI in 1937. The street decorations were designed by Mr Brian Tyler, a local architect.

visiting the gates. They would wait until a large group had formed and then took pictures of the scene, which were then transferred to postcards. These were displayed in shop windows and sold for a penny each. Many of these cards have survived and we are able to appreciate the amount of work put into creating these edifices, which only stayed in place for a few weeks.

THE EARLY 20TH CENTURY

The City in 1900

In the early years of the 20th century there was much to preoccupy the residents of the city. The death of Queen Victoria in January 1901, after 64 years on the throne, had left the whole nation with a sense of loss. Few could remember the time before her reign.

The Royal Sussex Regiment had been heavily involved in the Boer War. In 1899 the troops paraded through the streets, on their way to the station from the barracks, before embarking to fight in South Africa. Now the survivors were returning and several prominent local men had been lost. Dean Hannah's son, William, was killed, and Bishop Wilberforce's son was severely wounded in battle. In July 1901 a detachment of 90 men marched directly from the station, on their return, to the Cathedral to take part in a

A charming picture of North Street taken in 1870. The coachmen wait in the rain whilst their mistress shops.

Soldiers wait on Chichester Station to be taken to Southampton before embarking to South Africa. (*WRSO*)

Taken in 1898 this picture shows a military band from the Barracks marching down North Street. Seemingly they are led by a party of young boys.

The city's sewers being laid in South Street in 1898, the bowler hat was the traditional attire for a foreman at that time. (*WRSO*)

Chichester taxi owner, Mr Wellcome, had one of the first cars to be seen on the city's streets in 1910.

service of thanksgiving. They were accompanied by hundreds of citizens who, it was reported, trudged alongside and behind them, cheering all the way.

Work was still taking place around the city extending main drainage. Before 1896 there had been no sewers and most properties relied on cesspits. There had been much opposition to plans to provide drainage, the city council was divided between the 'drainers' and the 'non-drainers'. Finally a scheme was adopted after a report, in 1889, showing that the incidence of typhoid in the city was among the highest in the country, including London.

In 1904 Cicestrians watched the rebuilding of the old Oliver Whitby School in West Street, to a fine design by Sir Reginald Blomfield. In 1910 the first automobiles were to be seen in the streets of the city. It is said that the first local registration, PO1, was taken by Alderman Sharp Garland, the Chichester grocer.

Chichester Businesses
Most workers pursued their trades within the city boundaries. The traditional businesses of woolstapling, brewing and leatherworking together with the old established firm of Shippams continued to flourish and be the main sources of employment.

Woolstapling had taken place in Chichester since the 16th century. By 1900 the trade was centred in Tower Street where Ebenezer Prior had his business. Ebenezer, a former mayor of the city, had bought out the city's other stapling firm, Charles Parson and Son of the Pallant, in the 1890s. He sold his East Walls premises to Shippams and purchased the former Fighting Cocks public house in Tower Street as well as the adjoining Lancastrian School building when that establishment moved to new premises in Orchard Street. On the pub site he built a new three-storey building where, at shearing time, May and June, both local farmers and those as far away as

Devon and Somerset would deliver fleeces. These were broken up and sorted and graded into the various types and qualities before being packed into bales and sent to manufacturers. In its heyday in the 1920s, about 30 men worked in the business which survived World War Two and eventually closed in 1962.

Gibbings Harrison and Company were tanners whose business was established in Chichester in 1641. Their premises were by the River Lavant in Westgate on a site where tanning had been carried out since the 14th century. The company used an imprint of the Market Cross as their trade mark and the quality of the leather hides from Chichester was recognised throughout the industry. The conversion of hides into the finished article took between six months to a year depending on the thickness and colour of the hide.

Each day the process of tanning at Westgate used over a ton of oak bark, much of which originally came from local sources although latterly imported bark was used. Before 1939 the company used British hides but later these too had to be bought from abroad to meet demand. By the late 1960s tanneries throughout the country were closing in face of competition from rubber and synthetic materials. Gibbings Harrison ceased to trade in 1974. The county council now use the site as offices and retains the name of The Tannery.

Brewing had traditionally been almost a cottage industry. Many public houses and inns producing their own beverages. At the beginning of the 19th century larger companies began to supply ales to these premises. In about 1805 Chichester brewer, John Dearling, moved his business from premises in East Street to a site at the rear of Westgate House. He subsequently sold the brewery to the Humphrey family who, besides being prosperous maltsters, also owned the Unicorn Inn in Eastgate Square. The new owners rebuilt the brewery. At its reopening in

September 1811, they gave a feast in the new cellar, attended by over 250 people including the mayor and members of the Corporation. In 1827 the business was sold to George Henty, who already owned over 50 licensed houses. On his death in 1830 the business passed to his sons George and Robert. In 1850 they purchased the Spain Brewery in Petersfield and by 1851 the brewery was employing 22 men and boys. George became the sole proprietor in 1855 when he purchased his brother's share of the concern for £22,473.

The brewery suffered a catastrophic fire in 1865, but it was rebuilt in three years. The business continued to grow and by 1889 owned 149 public houses. In the same year the firm bought out the 100-year-old Gatehouse Brewery in South Street, with its 33 pubs, and became a limited company with a share capital of £150,000 employing over 200 staff.

In 1921 Henty's business amalgamated with that of George Constable, the owner of breweries in Arundel and Littlehampton, to form a new company trading as Henty and Constable Ltd. By 1928, when it took over Kinnel's brewery in Emsworth, it was one of the largest brewing companies in the south of England and the major employer in Chichester.

During the war years, brewing was considered an important industry and thousands of servicemen enjoyed Henty and Constable's beers. In 1954 the company's managing director and

This picture of East Street taken in 1963 shows Shippam's factory before its enlargement which took in the snack bar and Biffin's grocery store. The date of 1750 on its pediment – the factory was built in 1912 – refers to the company's establishment in the 18th century. (*C.N.J. Shippam*)

Queen Mary is seen talking to Mr A.E.C. Shippam on her visit to the factory on 29 July 1924. Also in the picture is Mr G.P. Shippam and Her Majesty's lady-in-waiting, Lady Seymour. The ex-servicemen among the workforce wore their campaign medals for the occasion. (*C.N.J. Shippam*)

principal shareholder Richard Iltid Henty died, at the age of 52, whilst cruising on the *Queen Mary*. The business had to be sold to meet death duties. The public houses were bought by Tamplins Brewers of Brighton, a subsidiary of the Watney Group, and Friary Holroyd Healy of Guildford. The brewery was closed, the plant and equipment being sold, much of it for scrap. Entrusted with this task was the last employee on the company pay roll, the former bottling manager, Arthur Green, the author's father. The premises were converted into a complex of light industrial units which were eventually demolished to make way for housing. The site's previous use and owners have been commemorated in the street names of Henty Gardens and The Maltings.

The family business of C. Shippam and Son was founded in Chichester in 1750. It was established by Shipston Shippam, lately Sergeant Shippam of His Majesty's 72nd Regiment of Foot. Shipston would send his 12-horse wagons around markets and fairs in the West Country, buying such provisions as butter, cheese and bacon. His business was located in premises opposite the brewery in Westgate. On Shipston's death, in 1778, his son Charles took over. He was able to gain valuable contracts to supply provisions to the Royal Navy at Portsmouth. Despite leasing land adjoining the Westgate site it proved insufficient to meet the growth of the business, new premises were found in North Street by the Cross. In 1873 a site was obtained

Workers line the road as the royal car leaves the factory following the Queen's visit. In the background can be seen the County Police Station, formerly the city's gaol. (*C.N.J. Shippam*)

In addition to their range of meat and fish pastes, Shippam's were also renowned for their pork sausages. In the early 1970s they made over 10,000lbs of sausages a week, however demand for space meant that production had to cease. This picture taken on Friday 23 January 1970 shows Mrs J. Baldwin packing the last batch of chipolatas to leave the factory. (*C.N.J. Shippam*)

in East Street which still forms part of the present factory. Charles' son, also named Charles, travelled by paddle steamer to America in 1882 to introduce Shippam's products to the New World. By the end of the 19th century the business was producing a wide range of foods, including such exotic fare as 'galantine of wild boar's head and pistachio kernels'. The company trademark of Chichester Cross was becoming internationally known.

In 1911 Shippam's products were included in Captain Scott's provisions on his ill-fated Antarctic expedition. In the same year further land was obtained and the factory was rebuilt, now extending along East Walls. A great occasion for Shippam's was the visit of Queen Mary in 1924. The company received a Royal Warrant from George VI in 1948, an honour repeated in 1955 by Elizabeth II.

In 1968 an American company, Underwood's from Boston, acquired a share in Shippam's business. They already owned Seniors, the manufacturers of a similar range of products as Shippam's. In 1974 they took over full control of the company. The following year they sold the business and, over the next decade, the ownership changed several times. At the time of writing Shippam's is a part of the company which markets the Princes range of foods, and there has been talk of the business leaving Chichester, after over 250 years in the city and moving to St Ives in Cornwall.

World War One

For Cicestrians, the first noticeable effect of the declaration of war in 1914 was the campaign for recruits. When the mayor, Mr Sharp Garland, was appointed the city recruiting officer, there was no shortage of men queuing at the gates of the barracks to join Kitchener's Army. This was despite images of local troops leaving to fight in the Boer War just 15 years earlier still fresh in many people's minds.

Chichester Barracks had been built in the early 19th century as a camp to accommodate Napoleonic French prisoners of war. In 1814

Before conscription came into force Major William Lushington of the Royal Sussex Regiment had recruited a battalion of men to serve in 'Kitchener's Army'. On 5 August 1914 they marched out of the city to serve in France. This picture of the men was sent back from the front.

soldiers from the Sussex Regiment moved in whilst waiting to embark for the Battle of Waterloo. When it received a royal warrant in 1832, the regiment became known as the Royal Sussex Regiment. In 1873 the barracks were extensively enlarged and Chichester became the regiment's garrison town.

After receiving a short basic training in drill and the use of arms the new soldiers, like their Boer War predecessors, left the city by train to embark from one of the Channel ports to France. Those members of the Chichester City Band that had not joined the regular army were enlisted

As the garrison of the Royal Sussex Regiment, the Barracks were the training camp for soldiers in two world wars.

A poster calling for volunteers for the 7th Battalion of the Royal Sussex Regiment.

The memorial remained in Eastgate until the 1950s when, with the names of the fallen from World War Two added, it was moved to the Litten Gardens in St Pancras.

into the local Territorial Army and, dressed in khaki uniforms, accompanied the troops on their march through the city.

By the end of hostilities in 1918 the Royal Sussex had take part in many of the major battles of the war, adding the names of the Marne, Mons, the Somme and Gallipoli to its battle honours.

Over 600 men from Chichester lost their lives in the war and, on 20 July 1921, a memorial bearing their names was erected in Eastgate Square. The ceremony was led by Field Marshal Sir William Robertson, the wartime Chief of General Staff.

The memorial was moved to its present position in the Litten Gardens, off St Pancras in 1958 when the names of those who fell in World War Two were added.

Crowds gather in Eastgate Square on the 20 July 1921 for the unveiling and dedication of the war memorial. The ceremony was led by Field Marshall Sir William Robertson, the wartime Chief of the General Staff.

The 7th and 8th Dukes

The 7th Duke of Richmond succeeded to the title in 1903, by which time he was 58 years old and a widower. He took a close interest in horseracing, serving as a steward of the Jockey Club. Under his administration Goodwood became one of the leading racecourses in the country, attracting the sobriquet of 'Glorious Goodwood'.

His son, the 8th Duke, the was born in 1870. After attending Oxford University, he joined the Royal Sussex Regiment before transferring to the Irish Guards. He retired, aged 43, with the rank of major in 1912. He was recalled at the outbreak of World War One. Following service in France and Belgium, whilst waiting with his regiment to embark to Gallipoli, he contracted polio. As a result he was restricted to using a wheelchair for the rest of his life. During the war he lost both his brother, Esme, and his second son. Like his father, he was 58 years old before he succeeded to the dukedom in 1928. He was immediately faced with the problems of death duties which forced him to sell an estate in Scotland, and some of his land at Goodwood, together with family paintings and other treasures. He died in 1935 and was succeeded by his third son, Frederick.

Cinemas

Sussex was one of the earliest places in the country to enjoy cinematograph film shows, or, as it came to be known, the cinema. Within three weeks of the inaugural showing of the new animated photographs in London, their first appearance outside the capital was on 25 March 1896 at the Pandora Gallery in Brighton. The first recorded public film performance in Chichester was on Boxing Day, Saturday 26 December 1896 when several short films were shown during a pantomime in the Corn Exchange in East Street.

The Corn Exchange, in addition to its commercial use as a corn and grain market, was

The Olympia cinema in Northgate also boasted a roller-skating rink.

used for a variety of events by local societies and others. Copies of the *Chichester Observer* of the time advertise concerts, plays, operas and flower shows among the attractions carried on there. Starting on 30 October 1899, for one week, Joseph Poole's shows included *Pooles's Kinematograph of Animated Photography*; admission prices ranged from 6d (2½p) to 2s 0d (10p) with half price for children. In 1901 Joseph's brother Charles showed films of Queen Victoria's funeral and film from South Africa of the Boer War.

Films continued to be shown periodically until 1910, when Charles Poole hired the Exchange for the regular showing of films, the hall was adapted and a cinematograph licence granted. It was the Poole brothers who introduced the novelty of locally-shot films into their programme and patrons were able to see such events as the Bosham Regatta and cricket

Poole's Cinema in East Street dressed for the coronation of George V in 1910. At this time the building was still in daytime use as the Corn Exchange.

EXCHANGE THEATRE CHICHESTER

'Phone 2407.

We are now equipped with "High Fidelity" the finest Sound System.

A TWO-FEATURE SHOW
CONTINUOUS DAILY
from 2 p.m. (Sundays 8 p.m.)

REDUCED MATINEE PRICES :
(Until 3.30) (Except Bank Holidays)

1/- - 9d. - 6d.

EVENING PRICES (From 3.30)—

**2/- — 1/6 — 1/-
9d. — 6d.**

Programmes Commence Approx.
2.0 — 4.50 — 7.40

Children at reduced prices, except Sundays, Saturdays and Bank Holidays.

Always a Good Show !

Sidney C. Lacey
LIMITED
85, East Street,
CHICHESTER

THE SUSSEX STATIONER

Printers, Booksellers, High Class Leather and Electro Plated Articles

A programme advertising the attractions to be shown at the Exchange during the first week of the war in September 1939.

matches played in Priory Park. At this time the premises were still in use for grain sales during the daytime and the cinema patrons were often seated on the corn bins around the perimeter of the hall. An article in the *Chichester Observer* in December 1910 stated: 'This is undoubtedly the most popular entertainment that has ever been presented to Cicestrians. An hour and a half at Poole's is an hour enjoyably spent'.

The success of Pooles' Picture Palace was soon noticed by local businessmen and, in 1911, the Olympia Electric Theatre opened at Northgate. It was advertised as being 'The most comfortable and up to date Electric Palace in the neighbourhood'. Prices for front seats were 3d, with back seats at 4d. It also offered live entertainment on the same bill as feature films and local films showing such items as employees of Henty's Brewery leaving work, and children from the Lancastrian Schools at play. The opportunity to see oneself or ones children on the screen proved irresistible and attracted large audiences. The proprietors of Poole's responded by introducing talent competitions offering a weekly prize of one guinea to the winner of the Saturday final. Performances at both cinemas continued throughout World War One, the official war film of the Battle of the Somme attracting large audiences in October 1916.

After the war, a third cinema was provided for the city when, in 1920, the Picturedrome was opened in South Street, this enterprise was the third such venture by Peter Stoneham an architect who had previously opened the Bognor Regis and Worthing Picturedromes. Access to the premises was a narrow doorway between Wren's Café and

The mayor, Councillor William Napper, attends the opening night of the Plaza Cinema in December 1936 accompanied by a full entourage of constables with staves, mace bearer and, on the right, the Town Clerk, Mr Eric Banks. (*Chichester City Council*)

Few pictures of the Picturedrome cinema exist, but it can be seen in the background of this picture of a band touring the city in 1927 to publicise a fête in the Bishop's Palace.

The Odeon Cinema in South Street in 1967.

Saunders' hardware shop with an additional entrance in West Pallant.

This competition had an adverse effect upon Poole's business. The new cinema offered better seating and used the latest projection equipment. In addition they poached the services of Poole's chief projectionist Bernard Mayer and their manager Natt Abatt. The proprietors of Poole's sold the business to Mr Stanley James, who restored the original name of the Corn Exchange to the cinema.

In February 1922 a fire, thought to have been caused by a customer's discarded cigarette, so devastated the Olympia that it did not recover. The building later became the Chichester garage of the Southdown Bus Company. Its distinctive front elevation can still be seen, as it is now used as a warehouse.

In 1927 the Corn Exchange was purchased by the Wainwright circuit who closed it down for four months so that it could be completely renovated. When it reopened in December it had been converted into a proper cinema. The front entrance had been redesigned, there were new seats, a new stage and new projection equipment. The name of the cinema was again changed,, it now became known just as the Exchange.

In August 1929 the Exchange caused great excitement among cinema-goers when it screened the first talking picture to be shown in West Sussex with *The Fox Movietone Follies* of 1929. Three weeks later the Picturedrome, which had been taken over by the County Cinema chain and renamed the Plaza, followed with *The Singing Fool* starring Al Jolson.

Early in 1936 the Gaumont-British Film Corporation announced that it was to build a new cinema on the site that it had acquired in Eastgate Square. By September the building was sufficiently advanced for the mayor, Councillor William Napper, to lay the foundation stone. The owners of the Plaza quickly responded by closing down in June for a complete reconstruction of the building. By the time they reopened in December the premises had been transformed beyond all recognition, the shops on either side of the entrance had been demolished, a café had been provided on the first floor and the auditorium had been revamped to provide a total of 1,063 seats. The opening was carried out by the mayor, the band of the 2nd Dragoon Guards played and a performance of Charles Laughton's new film, *Rembrandt* was screened, prior to its general release, for one night only.

Cicestrians had watched the building at Eastgate grow for over a year since the laying of the foundation stone. Finally, on 20 September 1937, the Gaumont Cinema was opened. It was a gala event, the opening carried out once again by Councillor Napper, accompanied this time by the Band of the Royal Marines and six Gaumont-British starlets. The film shown was *King Solomon's Mines*, with the added attraction of a newsreel of the recent world heavyweight contest between Henry Farr and Joe Louis. The new cinema had a total of 1,278 seats. Like the Plaza it contained a café but, uniquely, provided a car park for the use of its patrons.

The year 1939 marked the heyday of the cinema in Chichester. Despite being supplemented by members of the armed forces, business fell off during the war years. In truth the population of the city was not large enough to justify over 3,000 seats providing, between them, some 60 performances a week.

The names of the cinemas continued to change. In 1945 the Plaza was renamed the Odeon, and in 1948 the Exchange became known as the Granada Exchange. Two years later, in 1950, it became the Granada.

In February 1960 the Odeon was closed down, followed eight months later by the Gaumont. Thus, the Granada, successor to the city's first cinema, was the last to survive, which it did until 1980. As the number of patrons declined the owners, Granada, applied for the premises to be used as a bingo hall. Permission was refused and the cinema was closed. It now serves as a Macdonalds restaurant. The Gaumont was converted into a swimming pool, which survived until 1987 when the new Westgate Centre was opened. The Odeon building became the Fine Fare supermarket and is now occupied by Iceland.

In 1982, the Chichester Film Society was formed to bring films to Chichester and this still operates in the New Park Road Centre.

World War Two

On Saturday 29 April 1939, Portsmouth Football Club beat Wolverhampton Wanderers 4-1 to win the FA Cup. The club had many fans in Chichester but as they celebrated, air-raid sirens sounded over the city. For many this demonstration was the first time that the warning and all-clear tones had been experienced. It was not to be the last. Portsmouth, incidentally, were Cup holders for the next seven years, for the next Final was not to be until 1946.

The trial of the sirens was just one of the preparations that took place as the prospect of war became more likely. The City Council set up the local Civil Defence headquarters in their offices in North Street. Gas masks had been issued in 1938 and, during the early months of 1939, air-raid wardens were enlisted and trained to deal with the type of emergencies that might occur. A series of instructional leaflets

Greyfriars, the City Council Offices, seen in 1940 protected by a wall of sandbags.

concerning the precautions to be taken in the event of air-raids, gas attack and shortages of food were issued by the City Council and delivered to all households.

When, on 3 September 1939, war was declared on Germany, a well-prepared sequence of events was initiated. Ration books and identity cards were issued, every person being allocated their own personal identity number. Over the following months the appearance of the city changed radically. Air raid shelters were built in residential areas, large metal static water tanks were erected in the main streets to provide water to fight fires should the mains supply be broken. Road blocks and tank traps appeared throughout the city, blast walls were built over house windows. Householders saw their garden railings to be taken away to be melted down to make munitions. It was a pointless exercise; almost all metal salvaged throughout Britain in this way was not of a quality to be of any use in the war effort. Outside the Council offices in North Street a wall of sandbags was erected.

The decision to evacuate children from places thought to be at risk from attack by enemy bombers was made as early as 1938. The Ministry of Health was given the responsibility for supervising the scheme. Chichester was designated as one of the reception areas. Within a few days of the declaration of war train loads of children, with brown name labels attached to them, arrived at the railway station carrying their gas masks and cases containing their personal belongings. Officials with groups of children in tow walked the streets knocking at doors to find them billets. Mostly they were found homes without difficulty, although local authorities had powers to compulsorily allocate children if necessary.

The evacuees that were sent to Chichester came mostly from South London. In particular many came from Thornton Heath. Both the Boys' and Girls' High Schools found their numbers almost doubled when their premises were shared with evacuated pupils.

Following a broadcast appeal by the War Minister, Anthony Eden, in May 1940, many men between the ages of 17 and 65 came forward to join the newly-formed Local Defence Volunteers, the predecessors to the Home Guard.

A mother gives her son a last kiss before he joins the train taking him away to a place thought to be less at risk from enemy air raids.

The Observer Corps, the Special Constabulary and the Civil Defence also recruited those wishing to 'do their bit' towards the war effort. The wardens and the police were given the task of patrolling the streets at night to enforce the blackout regulations which affected both buildings and vehicles. Others were designated as fire wardens and spent nights keeping watch from such vantage points as the Bell Tower, the water tower of Graylingwell Hospital and the roof of Shippam's factory.

As shortages began to take effect word of imminent deliveries would be the signal for queues to gather quickly outside food stores. Housewives would run between Bunn's greengrocery and Byerley's the fishmongers in East Street and then maybe to Shippam's butcher's shop in South Street. The sight of

military personnel and vehicles in the streets became commonplace. Servicemen would often show shoulder flashes indicating that they were from occupied countries. Locally many were from Czechoslovakia and Poland, and serving with the RAF. Others from countries in what was then the British Empire, were to be seen among British troops.

Children, including the author, returning to St James's Infants School after the Easter holidays in 1941 were sent home with the news that the school had been requisitioned by the Royal Air Force. It was to be used as an operations room controlling aircraft movements in the West Sussex sector. Eventually the school was relocated to share premises with the St John's private school in the Hornet. Later in the war the school returned to its original home when the

Queues quickly formed outside Bunn's on the rumour of imminent deliveries of such delicacies as oranges or bananas.

control room was moved to larger accommodation in Bishop Otter College.

In the summer of 1941 the skies were criss-crossed with the white trails of fighter planes.

Today the derelict control tower of the Battle of Britain air station gives no clue as to the intense activity that went on here during the war years.

The Royal Air Force station at Tangmere was at the centre of the Battle of Britain. On 16 August 1940 the airfield had been bombed. The sound of explosions as bombs hit the concrete runways is not forgotten by those who were in Chichester that day. Fortunately, many satellite airfields had been located elsewhere in the area in order that aircraft should not be concentrated, and thus vulnerable to attack from the air. One of these was the Westhampnett Airfield, opened just before the Tangmere raid in 1940, and home of, among others, 502 Spitfire Squadron. This site was converted after the war into what is now the Goodwood motor racing circuit. Other satellite airfields were constructed at Merston, Apuldram, Selsey and Lagness near Bognor Regis.

In May 1942 there was a build up of Canadian troops in the West Sussex area. On 19 August

The SEA The FARM The FOREST

22 BYERLEY & Co 23

FISH MERCHANTS POULTERERS &c DEALERS of GAME

FREEMAN HAR

As their sign indicated, Byerleys's sold fish, poultry and game, making them an essential shop during wartime in Chichester.

CHRISTMAS DAY SERVICE

FOURTH CANADIAN FIELD REGIMENT
— ROYAL CANADIAN ARTILLERY —

BY PERMISSION OF RAPHAEL TUCK

in a . .

CATHEDRAL

Somewhere - in - England

DECEMBER 25th, 1942   09.45 HOURS

This service sheet for the Canadian troops' Christmas Day Service in 1942
'Somewhere in England' was hardly secret with a picture of the Cathedral
on the front cover.

that year, they took part in a seaborne raid on Dieppe. The raid was not a success. In September, German aircraft carried out a drop of thousands of leaflets, many landing over and around the city, showing photographs of the allied troops who had been killed or captured during the ill-fated raid.

Anti-aircraft gun emplacements were situated around the district. Bofors guns were installed, among other sites, in the allotments off Green Lane and in New Park Road Recreation Ground. In 1942 two 9ins Howitzers were placed in Oaklands Park, trained to fire on the Thorney RAF Station, eight miles away in case of invasion. As the threat of invasion diminished they were replaced by two 12ins guns set on railway wagons, each part of an artillery train comprising engine, ammunition wagons, a cookhouse wagon and accommodation coaches. One of these trains was stationed in a siding in the Chichester goods yard, the other on the spur line within the station yard that was part of the former Selsey Tramway. The soldiers were all billeted in the city, the officers in North Lodge at Northgate and the men in No.53 South Street.

Following the death of Major J.S. Courtauld, the city's MP, a by-election was held in May 1942, when Lancelot Joynson-Hicks, the National Government candidate, was elected. The new member was the son of the former Home Secretary, William Joynson-Hicks, later Lord Brentford.

Chichester did not suffer from air-raids to the same extent as many towns. It was bombed by the enemy on three occasions. All were thought to be random attacks aimed to disturb public morale rather than to strike at specific targets. The first of these, in 1942, saw houses in Basin Road destroyed in a daylight raid. These houses were never replaced and the site is now a car park. On 10 February 1943 the centre of the city was hit by several bombs which damaged buildings in Tower Street, North Street and St Martin's Street. The last raid took place during the night of 26 April 1944, another random attack, possibly by a returning plane that failed to reach its target, which struck at houses in Armadale and Bridge Roads.

The only other time that Chichester was in danger from the air was on the afternoon of 11 May 1944 when a four-engined American Liberator bomber, which had set out to bomb targets in occupied France prior to the D-Day landings, suffered an engine fire. The captain set the automatic pilot to take the plane out into the Channel and the crew baled out. But the fire affected the controls and the aircraft turned and headed back inland. It lost height and plunged towards the city, the bombs exploding when it was just above the Chichester Electric Laundry premises in Velyn Avenue.

The scene in Chapel Street after the daylight raid on Chichester in February 1943. (*WRSO*)

This smithy had stood in the Hornet for over 100 years when it was demolished by the American bomber that crashed there in May 1944. (*Frank Hellyer*)

In the early months of 1944 there was a build-up of troops in the area, prior to the invasion of Normandy. American Army personnel took over the former Theological College, now offices, on the corner of Westgate and Parklands Road. An airfield was built on farm land at Apuldram for squadrons of Typhoon aircraft who were engaged on bombing missions over Occupied France in preparation for the coming assault.

The part that was played by the harbours along the south coast in the construction of components for the Mulberry harbours has been well documented. What is often not appreciated is that much of the concrete used in the fabrication of these units was dug from the gravel pits around Chichester. For a period of 150 days from November 1943 over 4,000 tons of gravel daily were delivered, by 150 lorries working night and day, to the docks where construction was taking place. After D-Day, Hall

The residents of
Little London
celebrate the end
of the war with a
street party in
August 1945.

The mayor, Councillor Alice Eastland, takes the salute on St George's Day 1951. Traditionally, this is the day when the soldiers of the regiment exercise their privilege of marching through the city with bayonets fixed, a privilege granted to them when they were given the Freedom of the City in 1950. (*CCC*)

and Company's personnel were officially commended for the long hours that they worked arranging the quarrying and the delivery of materials under conditions of great secrecy.

Meanwhile a new peril was threatening from the sky. The German V1 flying bombs, popularly known as 'doodle bugs', were being sent from Northern Europe. Fortunately most fell in open country although many passed over Chichester on the way to their targets at Portsmouth.

When the cessation of hostilities was announced on 8 May 1945, VE day, the citizens made their way to the Market Cross. The city's traditional site for gathering was once again the scene of celebrations and locals were joined by representatives from allied armed forces. Today

Tangmere is the home of the Military Aviation Museum and includes a feature detailing the history of the station from its foundation in 1917 to its closure in 1970.

Bishop Bell

In 1929 George Kennedy Allen Bell was appointed Bishop of Chichester, a position he was to hold for nearly 30 years. Himself the son of a clergyman, Bell was born on Hayling Island in 1883, within sight of the Cathedral spire. He won a scholarship to Westminster School and from there, in 1901, gained a classical scholarship to Christchurch, Oxford. He excelled himself at Oxford, where among other distinctions, he won the prestigious Newdigate

Bishop Bell gives a blessing to a plough at the West Door to the Cathedral before the Plough Sunday service in August 1946. Over 500 members of local Young Farmers' Clubs attended.

Prize for poetry, a previous winner of which had been Oscar Wilde.

After study at Wells Theological College, George Bell was accepted as a deacon at Leeds Parish Church where he was ordained as a priest in 1907. His stay at Leeds was brief, for in 1910 he returned to his old college at Oxford, to teach classics. In 1914 he went to Lambeth as chaplain to Archbishop Davidson and, in 1924, was appointed Dean of Canterbury Cathedral.

When he became the 97th Bishop of Chichester, at the age of 46, he was one of the two youngest bishops in England. He soon launched a seven-year plan to build and aid churches, halls, schools and training colleges within the Diocese. When workers for the East Sussex County Council wrote to him, complaining that their employer would not allow them to join a trade union, he himself joined the National Union of Public Employees and was proud to carry his membership card for the rest of his life.

It was in the war years that Bishop Bell achieved national prominence when his speech in the House of Lords, against the saturation-bombing of German cities, was followed by a wave of unpopularity. He was the butt of cartoons and music-hall jokes. The fact that he had spoken out against Hitler and the Nazis since the early 1930s was ignored. In that time he had been responsible for bringing over 70 pastors of the German church, with their families, to the safety of England.

In 1942 the bishop was asked by the Ministry of Information to attend a meeting in Stockholm with Swedish churchmen. In fact this was a

In June 1954 Chichester's first female mayor, Alice Eastland, is pictured with Bishop Bell on the occasion of his receiving the Freedom of the City. Alice and her husband, Jesse, both served as mayor and were themselves given the same honour.

cover for him to meet representatives of the German resistance movement who wished to convey a message to the British Government concerning their activities. This was, of course, not known by the general public and many continued to revile him as a pacifist.

In 1944 when William Temple, the Archbishop of Canterbury, died Bell was widely expected to be appointed to replace him. However then, as now, the decision was made, not by members of the Church, but by the Prime Minister. Winston Churchill could not forget Bell's wartime forthrightness – the new Archbishop was Geoffrey Fisher.

Maybe the decision was fortunate, since the commitment of work as Archbishop may have prevented the bishop from taking his leading role in the ecumenical movement for church unity. In 1948 he was elected as the first chairman of the World Council of Churches. In this capacity he carried the name of Chichester to countries throughout the world.

In 1954, on the 25th anniversary of his consecration, the people of Chichester made their bishop a Freeman of the city. He retired in January 1958, after 29 years as bishop, to live in Canterbury. He died in October the same year, aged 75. Tributes to his life's work came from around the world and a memorial service in the Cathedral the following week was led by the Archbishop of Canterbury and attended by ecclesiastical and civic dignitaries. When the Arundel Screen in the Cathedral was restored in 1961 it was rededicated as the Bell-Arundel Screen as a memorial to Chichester's most renowned 20th-century bishop.

Changes to the city
Between the wars several major buildings were constructed in the neo-Georgian style considered appropriate for the city. These included East Street's National and Provincial Bank in 1929, now the premises of the Halifax Building Society. A few doors away, Marks and Spencer's

County Hall, the home of the West Sussex County Council in 1946. The circular structure in front of the building was a wartime static water tank.

shop was built in 1936, followed the next year by the Post Office in West Street.

In 1933 Cecil G. Stillman was appointed as the county architect. He was responsible for three outstanding public buildings in Chichester. They were the County Hall, completed in 1936, followed by St Richard's Hospital in 1937 and the County Court in Southgate in 1939.

A major project, commenced in 1938 and completed in the 1950s was the Chichester bypass. It is now hard to imagine that, prior to its construction, the main A27 coastal trunk road ran through the city, including passing through the notorious Westgate 'bottleneck' and around the Cross.

The West Sussex County Council built St Richard's Hospital in 1937 as a long-stay establishment for the handicapped and elderly. It was opened in August 1939. Within a month, the country was at war and the Ministry of Health designated St Richard's as a general hospital. In 1940, ten 40-bed hutted wards were built, bringing the hospital's bed complement to 594.

During the same period Eastgate Square was the site of two major projects. The Gaumont Cinema was built in 1937 and a year later the 17th-century Unicorn Inn was demolished. The distinctive rounded front to the Gaumont building was reflected in the design of the new Unicorn. The inn closed for business in 1960 and the premises were used by the Festival Theatre as additional accommodation. After extensive modification in 1990, the building is now the offices of the *Chichester Observer*.

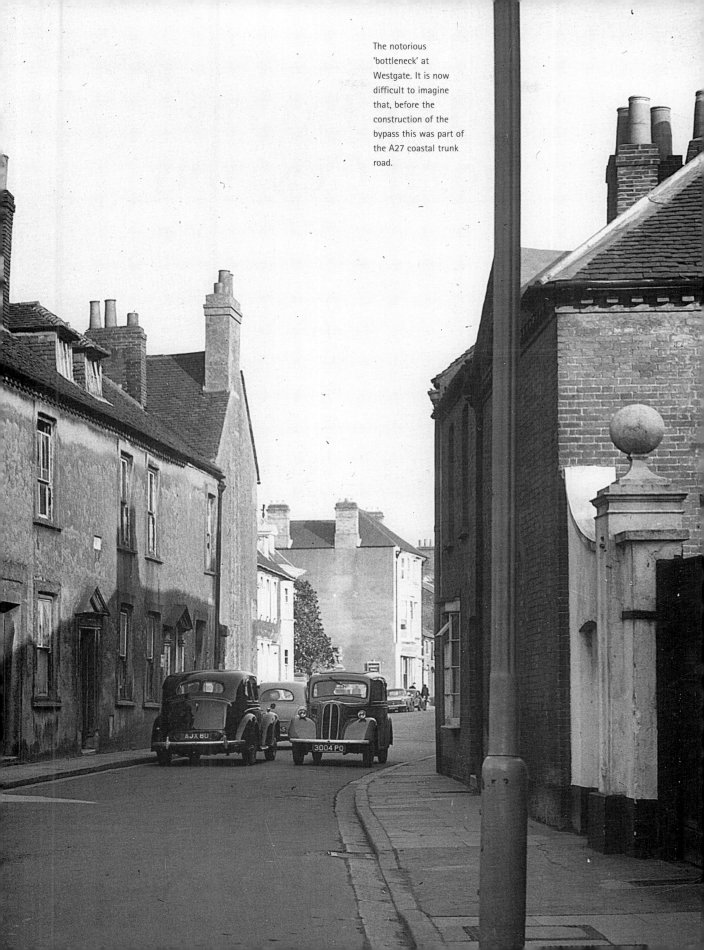

The notorious 'bottleneck' at Westgate. It is now difficult to imagine that, before the construction of the bypass this was part of the A27 coastal trunk road.

THE LATTER 20TH CENTURY

IN 1950 a visitor to Chichester would have found a city that, despite two world wars, had changed little since the early years of the century. There had been residential developments on the outskirts and some changes, mentioned previously, had taken place affecting the high streets, but nothing compared to the transformations that took place in the succeeding 50 years.

Many people still work in the city centre, but the nature of the work has changed. Except, perhaps, for Shippams, manual work has generally moved to the industrial estates. Garages and petrol stations which once traded in the main streets have moved out of the city. There has been an increase in the numbers employed in the service industries and in shops. The fine residential properties in the Pallants are now the offices of professionals and the city is home to several publishing houses.

In the years following the war, the city council were responsible for building three housing

Before 1960 many garages and car showrooms were to be found in the main streets. All the buildings in this 1959 picture of Southgate have since been demolished to make way for office development.

Chichester railway station was built in 1961 to a design by the British Railways Southern Region Architect's Department. Many thought that the city deserved better; it cannot be said to have improved with age. (*Charles Attwell Collection*)

estates, at Whyke, Parklands and in the meadows off Spitalfields Lane, where prefabricated factory-built houses made by the Orlit Company were erected. The demolition of Somerstown has been mentioned earlier. Private house building was restricted until the early 1960s. Once controls were lifted new developments sprang up in and around the city. The largest of these is the East Broyle Estate on former farm land off St Paul's Road. A feature of current new development is the amount of accommodation being provided for the elderly, the former gas works site and other nearby locations have been built on, with flats and housing for this purpose.

In 1966 Chichester was chosen, together with the cities of Bath, Chester and York to be the subject of studies, commissioned by the Minister of Housing, to discover how old towns could be reconciled to modern needs whilst retaining their architectural and historic values. As a result of these studies changes were made to the laws concerning the conservation of historic buildings and the designation of conservation areas. Today the area inside the city walls is so designated, and many buildings have 'listed' category.

No part of the city has seen more change in recent years than the Southgate area. The former County Police Station, made redundant when the new station was built in 1935, was finally demolished in 1954 and replaced by the Southdown Bus Station. The old railway station, built in 1840, was also pulled down in 1961 to make way for the present structure, designed by British Railway's Architects' Department. Several

Above: North Street in 1962, showing why pedestrianisation became necessary. Below: East Street in 1962.

The new library built to a circular design, under construction in 1967.

premises, including Wadham's car showrooms and the Green Parrot café were replaced by the City Gates office building. The area was further changed in 1965 when buildings were demolished to make way for the new ring road.

As the city's population has grown, additional facilities to cater for the increase have been provided. A new public library was opened in Tower Street in 1967, to a design by the County Architect, F.R.Steele. In 1971 the Chichester Crematorium was built on the site of an old gravel pit. The Westgate Centre has been built to provide recreational opportunities and the College of Technology caters for educational needs

In 1976 parts of North Street, East Street and South Street were pedestrianised. The scheme entailed major works to provide rear delivery access for the high street shops. Although some traders were initially concerned about the possible effect of the proposal upon their businesses, few would wish to return to the days when cars and lorries obstructed the streets.

Developments at Goodwood

The 9th Duke of Richmond had a passion for motor cars and, on coming down from the university in the 1920s, he worked on the shop floor at the Bentley factory. He competed in motor racing events under the name of 'Freddie' March, winning races at Brooklands and on the Isle of Man. The death of his father, only seven years after succeeding to the title, meant that the new duke had to meet death duties before the

The start of a 500cc race in 1950, on the former wartime aerodrome which was adapted as a motor racing circuit by the Duke of Richmond.

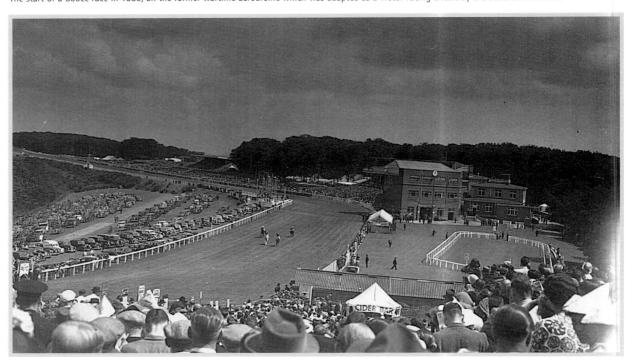

The finish of a race in the 1952 horse racing meeting seen from the popular Trundle enclosure.

With Goodwood House in the background, a dragster commences its run at the 2001 Festival of Speed. (*Garry Long*)

family had time to recover from those of his grandfather. He disposed of Scottish estates that had been in the family's possession for hundreds of years. In 1948 he started motor racing on the former wartime fighter airfield at Westhampnett. For 18 years the Goodwood motor racing circuit attracted the world's top drivers. In 1966, faced with the need for expensive safety precautions, racing had to cease. After the war the duke formed the Goodwood Estate Company to control the various businesses of the estate. He died in 1989 aged 85.

The 10th – and present - Duke is qualified as a chartered accountant and is also a distinguished churchman, having represented the Diocese of Chichester on the general synod of the Church of England and serving as a Church Commissioner. Like his ancestors he takes a prominent part in local affairs. He has been

Chancellor of Sussex University and President of the Sussex County Cricket Club. The Duchess of Richmond has been instrumental in introducing international dressage events to Goodwood. The duke, following the lead of his father, has handed the management of Goodwood to his son, the Earl of March who has recently staged the annual Goodwood Festival of Speed on the estate.

The Festival Theatre

Since 1962 Chichester has possessed an internationally-renowned theatre. In the 40 years since the Chichester Festival Theatre opened, many of the country's leading actors, actresses and stage performers have appeared on its thrust stage. The theatre was built as the result of one man's inspiration, a man who had the necessary energy and vision to put his dream into practice.

A present-day view of the theatre.

In November 1961, as the theatre nears completion, Sir Lawrence Olivier joins the workmen in a 'topping out' drink.

HRH Princess Alexandra stands back to read the inscription after laying the foundation stone of the Festival Theatre in May 1961.

The founder of the theatre, Leslie Evershed-Martin, has told the story of how, one evening in January 1959, he was watching the BBC's *Monitor* arts programme on television. An item that was shown about the theatre in Stratford, Ontario, captivated his attention. The people of this remote Canadian town, roughly the size of Chichester, had built themselves a theatre that was enticing the finest actors to appear under the direction of Tyrone Guthrie (later Sir Tyrone), the renowned theatrical producer.

Mr Evershed-Martin had long been associated with Chichester, having practised as an optician in the city since 1932. He served for 18 years as a city councillor, twice standing as mayor. During his term in office he had been instrumental in founding the Eventide Home for the elderly at Donnington. In 1956 he had instituted the city's annual Gala-Day.

Having decided that Chichester should have a theatre Evershed-Martin first identified a suitable site at Oaklands Park, the site of the annual Sloe Fair, which was owned by the city council. He next approached Tyrone Guthrie, who he persuaded to give his support to the scheme and contacted many of the most influential people in the area gaining further backing. As a result, a committee was formed and architects commissioned to produce plans for a theatre.

The architects chosen were Powell and Moya, the partnership that had received praise in 1951 for the design of the Skylon, the prize-winning structure that was symbol of the Festival of Britain. Philip Powell had a connection with Chichester in that his father was a canon of the Cathedral.

They produced a unique hexagonal-shaped design for the building, to be constructed of reinforced concrete, with the underside of the stepped auditorium visible externally. The space underneath the auditorium contained the entrance foyer, dressing rooms, etc. Instead of the traditional proscenium arch stage, a thrust stage – which extends into the auditorium and is surrounded by the audience on three sides – was adopted.

Building work started in 1961 and Princess Alexandra laid the foundation stone on 12 May. One year later, on 3 May 1962, the builders, McAlpines, handed over the completed theatre which had cost £110,000.

Other commitments prevented Tyrone Guthrie from becoming the Festival Theatre's first director. Evershed-Martin approached Sir Laurence Olivier who accepted the post. He

proved to be an inspired choice. The play chosen by Sir Laurence for the first production on 5 July 1962 was *The Chances*, by Jon Fletcher. The cast included Kathleen Harrison, Keith Michell, John Neville and Joan Plowright.

During its first season, the theatre became a popular venue for members of the Royal Family, and Princess Margaret and the Earl of Snowdon were early visitors. The Queen and Prince Philip came to a gala performance in July when Sir Laurence appeared in *Uncle Vanya*.

Since the first night, the cream of British theatre has appeared on the thrust stage. The theatre has been a major success story that may never have happened had Leslie Evershed-Martin not switched on his television set that evening in 1959.

Leslie Evershed-Martin, the theatre's founder, leads a party of visitors, including the mayor, John Selsby (third from right), to view the nearly-completed building in February 1962.

The Town Clerk, Eric Banks, the mayor, Alderman Charles Newell, the mayor of Chartres, Monsieur Pichard, all pictured in the Chichester Council Chamber on the occasion of the signing of the deed of twinning with Chartres on 28 February 1959. (*Anne Sclicuna*)

Chichester and Chartres

The Association of Le Monde Bilingue was formed in France after World War Two to encourage the forming of alliances between people of different countries. In February 1959, under a scheme promoted by the Association, Chichester became 'twinned' with the French city of Chartres.

The two cities share much in common. They are of comparable size and population, they both have cathedrals and were both walled communities in the Middle Ages. The twinning has resulted in sporting, cultural and educational groups making exchange visits.

In effect, three communities became triplets

The deputy mayor of Ravenna, the mayor of Chartres, George Lemoine, with Chichester mayor, John Wilton, meeting in Chartres in 1992. At that time Chartres was twinned with both Chichester and Ravenna. Chichester twinned with the Italian city in 1996. (*John Wilton*)

when, in November 1996, Chichester became twinned with Ravenna in Italy, a city that had become a twin with Chartres in 1990.

In recognition of the alliances, the City Council have named parts of the ring road Avenue de Chartres, and Via Ravenna. In Chartres the authorities reciprocated by creating the Rue de Chichester.

The twin relationship was further cemented in 1998 when Chichester's Bishop Eric Kemp was appointed as an honorary canon, Chanoine d'Honneur, of Chartres Cathedral. In November 2000 Canon François Legaux, formerly Rector of Chartres Cathedral was installed as a canon in Chichester Cathedral.

Council Reorganisation

In 1974, the structure of local government was changed. Under the 1972 Local Goverment Act,

Chichester District Council was formed and Chichester City Council, together with the Rural District Councils of Chichester, Midhurst and Petworth, were abolished. Chichester became the administrative centre for the new authority.

It was proposed that, when the city council was ended, the citizens would have representatives on the new district council but no parish council. The city council petitioned to be allowed to become a 'successor parish council,' thus enabling it to retain its mayor and corporation. The mayor, Councillor Peter Weston, made an appeal to the Minister of Local Government and he was supported by the former County Archivist, Francis Steer, who put forward a strong argument based on historical precedents.

At this point a Chichester housewife, Mrs Phyllis Bransgrove, was feeling strongly about the government decision. She decided that,

A fine picture of the City Council in procession taken in May 1965 as they leave the Council House in North Street. Proceeded by his constables and the mace, the mayor is followed by the town clerk, the aldermen and councillors.

rather than wait for somebody to take action, she, herself, should do so. Mrs Bransgrove started a petition, and persuaded the bishop to be among the first to sign it. After sitting at a table outside the Assembly Rooms and making a door-to-door canvas she obtained over 3,000 signatures within the first two weeks.

In November 1973 the Boundary Commission, having taken into account the strength of local opinion, relented. They agreed that, because of its standing as one of the most ancient boroughs in the country, the city should be allowed to retain its council and its mayor, thus ensuring the survival of nearly 900 years of tradition. Mrs Bransgrove's contribution was recognised in 1989 when she received a civic award from the Council.

St Wilfrid's Hospice

In 1981 two groups of people, one in Bognor Regis the other in Chichester, who had both been working since the late 1970s with the aim of providing a hospice in the area south of the Downs, joined together to form the St Wilfrid's Hospice Charity. A site was found on land in Grosvenor Road, Chichester and plans were prepared. At a meeting in October 1984 an appeal was launched by the Duchess of Norfolk for £500,000. The scheme caught the imagination of people throughout the District and support groups were formed in many of the outlying villages.

Even those most closely associated with the appeal were surprised with the speed of the project. The building was commenced in June 1986 when the Duchess laid the foundation stone and, by October, the project's architect, Mr Terry Roberts, was able to hand over the keys of the completed building to Mr Laurie Thefaut, the appeal's chairman.

Furniture and equipment were purchased, staff were appointed and trained so that the first

The building of the hospice has been one of the city's modern success stories. (*Terry Roberts*)

patients were able to arrive in January 1987. By 1993 the success of the institution was such that it required an extension. St Wilfrid's is today an important and appreciated facility looking after people in the community suffering from terminal cancer or motor neurone disease. It achieves the best possible care and quality of life for patients and their families. No charges are made to patients and volunteer workers have, from the start, provided essential back-up to the professional staff. Local organisations, fund-raisers and charity shops raise the considerable funds needed to keep the Hospice running. St Wilfrid's has been one of Chichester's greatest success stories in recent years.

Chichester Cathedral in 2002

If, through daily familiarity, the splendours of Chichester Cathedral sometimes become commonplace the author recommends that you revisit and remind yourself of its special nature.

Almost certainly you will discover some feature or artistic treasure that has not been previously savoured.

In 2002 one is immediately impressed by a recent addition – the imposing statue of St Richard, placed on the concourse before the Bell Tower. Seemingly guarding the approach to the Cathedral's west door. The saint's fingers are raised in a blessing, yet his face is turned away from those receiving his benediction.

When making a visit, the poet Philip Larkin was so moved by the tomb of Richard Fitzalan, 13th Earl of Arundel and his second wife, Eleanor that he wrote the unforgettable poem *An Arundel Tomb* which begins 'Side by side, their faces blurred, the earl and countess lie in stone'. Equally memorable is the last line 'What will survive of us is love'. The tomb was brought to the Cathedral from Lewes Priory in 1538. Originally, though, their hands were not joined; they were linked during an 19th-century restoration.

The Duke and Duchess 'hand-in-hand' as made famous in Larkin's poem.

Dean Walter Hussey seen with the famous American composer Leonard Bernstein on his visit to Chichester in July 1965.

The first modern work to decorate the Cathedral was a painting by the German muralist Hans Feibusch depicting the baptism of Christ. It is said that the Chapter were not altogether happy with the work but as it had been donated by Bishop Bell they felt unable to refuse it. Today it is displayed on the west wall besides John Skelton's font, carved from Cornish stone and lined in beaten copper installed and dedicated in 1983.

Thanks to the enlightened stewardship of Dean Walter Hussey, from 1955 to 1977, there are many 20th-century works of art juxtaposed with the Cathedral's mediaeval glories. From the 14th-century choir stalls, decorated with misericords designed to support aged clerics, one can view the imposing and colourful tapestry, designed by John Piper and woven in France. Near to the mediaeval carved *Chichester Reliefs* in the south choir aisle wall, is the Mary Magdalene Chapel with Graham Sutherland's painting *Noli me tangere*, originally a controversial choice, now accepted for the great work of art that it is.

In 1965, Dean Hussey invited Leonard Bernstein to compose a piece of music for that year's Southern Cathedrals' Festival. As a result, the *Chichester Psalms* have become a established work in concert repertoire.

Dean Hussey's last commission, and not to be missed, was Marc Chagall's stained glass window, depicting *Psalm 150*, in the north retrochoir which was unveiled by the Duchess of Kent in 1978.

In the Cathedral, art and liturgy combine. Having relished the former, visitors may attend choral evensong and listen to the music of the organ and the Cathedral choir, when these elements blend to provide a deeply moving experience.

Chichester Festivities

In 1975 a three-day festival took place to celebrate the 900th anniversary of the Cathedral. As a result of the success of the event the Chichester Festivities have been held every year since. Taking place in July, the festival now extends over 18 days and includes Cathedral concerts, exhibitions lectures and other events. These attract international symphony orchestras, soloists and artists to take part in what is now one of the most important festivals in the south of England. It now traditionally culminates in a concert and fireworks display at Goodwood Racecourse.

The River Lavant

Little mention has been made in the preceding pages of Chichester's river, the Lavant. In the last decade it has made its presence felt in dramatic fashion. The river, rising at the foot of the Downs in the village of East Dean, runs through Singleton and Lavant, through fields east of Graylingwell before turning towards Chichester at Westhampnett. On reaching the city, it then skirts the south walls of the city and thence to the harbour at Apuldram.

The Lavant flows only in the winter months.

Young visitors admire a statue in the Cathedral's Paradise exhibition. (*Chichester Festivities Committee*)

The Sussex Central School was erected in 1812 in New Park Road, then known as Litten Road. It is shown here in 1868 when the River Lavant flooded. (*Garry Long*)

It is thought that, originally, it may have continued south to join the sea at Pagham. In Roman times there were two streams, between which the city was founded. When these streams were joined and diverted around the walls is unclear, possibly by the Romans at the time that the walls were built.

The river has regularly overflowed its banks and caused flooding, particularly in the St Pancras area. Spershott mentions floods in 1763 which extended as far as the north gate, as 'the same as in 1713'. He later wrote that the flood in 1771 was deeper than the 'beds of the wagons'. Other records tell of flooding in 1797 and 1809 and, in 1826, the *Brighton Herald* reported the 'filling of the cellars of more than half the houses in the city'. In the present century the

river burst its bank by the Green Lane footbridge in 1938 and again in 1960 when the bridge disappeared under the fast flowing water.

The Lavant made headline news when, in January 1994, the volume of water coming from the Downs was more than the culverts under Eastgate Square could take. After record autumn rainfall more than eight inches of rain fell during the fortnight following Christmas. Parts of the Hornet and St Pancras were under several feet of water and, at Westhampnett , floodwater covered the main road and flooded the site of the Sainsbury's supermarket, which had been destroyed by fire only a couple of months previously.

A national newspaper showed photographs of windsurfers sailing along the A27. Over 150,000 sandbags were provided by the local authorities

The 'river' seen in this picture is in fact the main road at Westhampnett roundabout. Army engineers erected the Bailey bridge over the road when water from the Lavant was diverted to nearby gravel pits. (*Garry Long*)

A 'Green Goddess' fire engine outside of Cover's shop in the Hornet.

A mass of hosepipes carry the pumped floodwater through the city to rejoin the Lavant further downstream. (*Garry Long*)

When the threat of flooding reappeared in November 2000, a well-prepared plan went into action. These pipes at Westhampnett carried millions of gallons away from the city. (*Garry Long*)

to protect threatened homes. More than 20 'Green Goddess' fire appliances were provided by the Home Office to supplement the County Fire Brigade's equipment. Heavy duty pumps were installed in Rowe's Garage site in the Hornet, recently demolished, sending as much as six million gallons of water a day through three miles of hose pipes around the city, to be discharged to the canal basin or back into the Lavant at Southgate. The army were called in to help and Royal Engineers erected Bailey bridges over the roads at Westhampnett roundabout and on the A259 at Merston. At the height of the emergency the RNLI were on standby at County Hall with inflatable lifeboats

Following the floods, plans were prepared for action should the floods reoccur. These were put into action sooner than expected for, in

In October 1993, Sainsbury's supermarket caught fire. It was rebuilt within 10 months and the new store opened in August 1994.

November 2000, the river level rose again. Within hours the pumps were back and householders awoke to find that a line of pipes and hoses had been put into place overnight to take the water away.

At Westhampnett, pumps capable of handling thousands of gallons an hour were installed, pumping the floodwater into nearby gravel pits from which it was routed away from the city and to the sea at Pagham. A multi-million pound relief scheme has now been commenced to provide permanent protection from the flooding that has periodically endangered Chichester for hundreds of years.

THE FUTURE

IN THE early years of the 21st century, there are many plans that promise an exciting future for the city. The German BMW company have chosen a site near Goodwood to build a new factory for the building of Rolls-Royce cars, where they are to employ over 350 workers. The South Downs are to be designated as a National Park, and it is hoped that this will enable the recreational opportunities of the Downs to be exploited, at the same time ensuring the protection of the landscape.

At the time of writing (May 2002) a scheme for the building of over 2,500 houses on land to the south of the A27 at Donnington has been put forward, with another 1,000 on a site to the east of the city. The implications of such an increase to the population of the city, at present about 26,000, on the facilities and infrastructure will present challenges to local authorities.

The redevelopment of the Girl's High School site in Stockbridge Road will provide a leisure complex including a multiplex cinema, a bowling alley, a hotel and new pubs and restaurants. The sale is intended to provide funds for extensive enlargements to the school's accommodation on its Kingsham campus.

In 2001 the Right Reverend John Hind was installed as the 100th Bishop of Chichester. He probably faces greater challenges than did his predecessors in promoting the Faith in the diocese, the boundaries of which are still those of the kingdom of the South Saxons.

A final picture of a scene that combines elements that have formed the basis of Chichester's history – the Market, the Church and the Corporation. In January 2002, to mark the 500th anniversary of the gift of the cross to the city by Bishop Storey, the ceremony was re-enacted. Seen in this picture are the mayor, Councillor Michael Shone, his chaplain, the Bishop, the Rt Revd John Hind, the town crier and the town clerk, Rodney Duggau. (*Gill Schone*)

A SELECTION OF FURTHER READING

Bathurst, David *The Selsey Tram* Phillimore, 1992.

Down, Alex. et al *Chichester Excavations, books 1 to 9* Phillimore, 1970–85.

Green, Ken *The Street Names of Chichester* Verdant Publications, 1997.

Hobbs, Mary (Editor) *Chichester Cathedral, An Historical Survey* Phillimore, 1994.

Hopper, Barone C. *100 years of Sanctuary, Graylingwell Hospital 1897–1997* Hopper, 1997.

Houlter, Graham *Sussex Breweries* SB Publications, 2001.

Keating, Leslie *The Book of Chichester* Barracuda Books, 1979.

Morgan, Roy *Chichester, A Documentary History* Phillimore, 1992.

Morris, David *The Honour of Richmond* Sessions of York, 2000.

Newbury, Ken *The River Lavant* Phillimore, 2000.

Poulson, Rumble & Smith *Sussex Police Forces* Middleton Press, 1987.

Price, Bernard *Bygone Chichester* Phillimore, 1975.

Price, Bernard *Chichester: The Valiant Years* Phillimore, 1978.

Price, Bernard *Changing Chichester* Phillimore, 1982.

Thomas, Emlyn *Georgian Chichester*, vols I,II & III Emlyn Thomas, 2001.

Vine, Paul *West Sussex Waterways* Middleton Press, 1985.

Warne, H. & T. Brighton *A Portrait of Bishop Otter College* WSIHE, 1992.

INDEX

Hurdis, James 51
Huskisson, William 102
Iron Age 13
Isle of Wight 22, 24, 29
Itchenor 32, 94, 96
Jackson, William 35, 73-4
Jacobite Rebellion 69
James, Stanley 133
Joynson, William 139
Juxon, William 51, 58-9
Juxon Close 59
Kainesham, William of 43
Kean, Edmund 83-4
Kenny, James 6, 23
Kent, Duchess of 162
Kéroualle, Louise de 67
Kingley Vale 25
Kingsham 24, 43, 167
Lady Holt Wood 72
Lady March 68
Lagness 137
Lancastrian Schools 123, 131
Lanfranc 26
Larkin, Philip 160
Lavant 9, 43, 55, 98-9, 123, 162-5, 168
Legaux, Canon François 158
Legion, Augusta 22
Lennox, Lady Sarah 71
Lenthall, Mr 58
Lewkenor, Christopher 55
Litten Cemetery 71
Litten Gardens 18, 129
Little London 62, 115, 141
Littlehampton 124
Local Defence Volunteers 135
Lord Brentford 139
Lord Cadogan 68
Lord Wilton 102
Lower Palaeolithic Age 10
Madlock, Robert 62
Maidenhith, John de 33
Malmesbury, William of 26
March, Earl of 67, 89, 153
Market Cross 9, 49-51, 53, 110, 123, 142
Market House 9, 50, 111
Marsh, John 83

Mary Magdalene Chapel 161
Mayer, Bernard 133
Mercia 24
Merricks, Alderman Samuel 115
Merston 24, 137, 165
Michell, Keith 156
Middle Ages 32, 53, 55, 57, 59, 157
Midhurst 9, 12, 31, 55, 57, 73, 93, 96, 99, 158
Midhurst, Stephen de 31
Midhurst Line, The 96
Military Aviation Museum 142
Mills, Richard 73
Monastery, Dominican 35
Monmouth, Duke of 92
Montgomery, Roger de 26, 28
Morley, Sir William 55-6
Morris, Roger 63, 68, 168
Mundham 24, 66
Murray, Dr 107
Murray, Miss K.M.E. 107
Murray, Mr 39-40
Napper, Councillor William 132, 134
Nash, John 110-11
Neolithic Man 8, 12
Nero 16, 22
Neville, John 156
New Park Road 71, 134, 139, 163
New Park Road Recreation Ground 139
Norfolk, Duchess of 159
Norman Conquest 8, 25-6, 31, 107, 140
North Lodge 139
North Pallant 83
North Street 9, 15-17, 19, 25, 45-6, 50, 53, 62-3, 68, 70-1, 90, 92, 110, 112, 120-1, 125, 134-5, 139, 150-1, 158
Northgate 46, 85, 130-1, 139
Noviomagus Regnensium 16, 18, 23
Nutbourne 24
Oaklands Park 139, 155
Oliver Whitby School 9, 65-6, 123
Olivier, Sir Laurence 156
Olympia Electric Theatre 131
Orchard Street 123
Otter, William 105-6
Oving 24
Oxmarket 45